THE VOICE WITHIN

Books by the same author

LOVE UNVEILED
LOVE IS GREEN
(as Margaret Baker)

POEMS TO TELL MY FRIENDS
(as Margaret Ayton)

THE VOICE WITHIN

MARGARET AYTON

A COLLECTION OF
INSPIRATIONAL POETRY AND THOUGHTS

With black and white photographs by the author

Best Wishes
Margaret Ayton

PILGRIM BOOKS
TASBURGH NORWICH ENGLAND

British Library Cataloguing in Publication Data
Ayton, Margaret
The voice within: a collection of inspirational poetry and thoughts.
I. Title
821′.914 PR6051.Y/

ISBN 0–946259–21–6

Photoset by Waveney Typesetters, Norwich
and printed in Great Britain by Oxford University Press

This book is dedicated to
the inspiring love and work
at the Cancer Help Centre, Bristol

With many thanks
for their support, loyalty and encouragement
to my husband Mike and the very persuasive
June Blythe and Glyn Kent-Davies

Grants from the
Russell Trust and the
Duffield Trust have
assisted with publication

CONTENTS

THE VOICE WITHIN 1
Love is . . .

LIFE IS LIKE A RAINBOW 5
Words – Love the sculptor – Harvest rhythm

LOVE UNVEILED 9
Love unveiled – I am nothing – Love is giving – Magic – Love aborted – The path to love – Missing you – New love – Under your spell – Sharing love – Romantic interlude

RELATIONSHIPS 21
This man that I love – Good friends – Teacher retiring – A new era – Unconditional love – S.O.S. – Lament of a tennis widow – The most precious things in life – Give and take

UNHAPPINESS 31
Neglected heart – Equine spirit – A blade of grass – Learning to love – Who cares? – Oasis in rejection – Reach out for me – The man in the park – Hope

SPIRITUAL GROWTH 43
Spiritual strength – Prayer – Seeds of love – The waters of life – A new beginning – Giving – Behold my Master – Unrivalled treasure

DESPAIR 55
Restlessness – Confession – Spider's web – Struggle – The tangled mind of a mentally disturbed woman – Butterfly – Morning light, Lake Coniston

PERSONAL EFFORT 67
Love is fragile – Man is a thief – Think two – To be loved – The observer – Grow your own love – The quality of life – The search

DISAPPOINTMENT 79
Trust – Cry wolf – Anxiety – Thinking of you – Freedom – In sympathy with a sea anemone – Learning

MOURNING 87
In Nature's arms I rest – Remember me – In memory of a friend – Death of a cat – Love lost – Another time, another place – Remembrance – The shell lives on – Thoughts from Hollie – The wings of freedom – Memories

DETERMINATION 99
Beginnings – The breath of love – My love for you – Light in the darkness – Awakening

TIME TO THINK 105
Morning greeting – A secret place – An afternoon in the Dales – Hymn to Wales – The Marble Quarry, Iona – Changes – Time on the beach – England – Tarn Hows – Continuation . . . – Benediction

POSITIVE THOUGHT AND ILLNESS 119
Island peace – Isle of Harris – Awareness – Pain –The view beyond my pain – View from a hospital window – Jean McCleod – The X-ray – The forgotten ones – Signs of Spring

LOVE IS GREEN 131
Love is green – Garden colours – Paradise – The bridle path in winter – Yorkshire walls – Rain in the Dales – Brooke Churchyard – Cormorants – Fionnphort – Fingal's Cave – Isle of Eriska – Glensanda – Journey from Stornoway – Scarista – Toe Head – The ferry pilgrims – The bat

WHO AM I? 153

INDEX 156

THE CANCER HELP CENTRE, BRISTOL

If you ask people to name the disease they most fear, you will almost always be told 'cancer'. The diagnosis can come like a thunderbolt, blowing apart life as we know it; and one of the worst aspects is the feeling there is nothing you can do to help yourself.

The Cancer Help Centre opened in 1980 to assist patients cope with their fears and anxieties, and teach them how to fight for their lives. It offers a special, self-help therapy that they can start at home after returning from treatment in hospital.

Patients at the Centre are encouraged to adopt a wholefood diet to boost their general health; they are taught stress control and relaxation to calm their anxieties, and given psychological counselling to help solve any personal problems that may be causing unhappiness and stress. Healing is given at a physical and spiritual level.

The therapy does not conflict in any way with standard medical treatments, but works alongside them to enhance their efficiency. It has won widespread support from the medical profession and is being thoroughly researched by the Imperial Cancer Research Fund.

Patients come from all over the world and can choose to stay for a week or more, or just one day. The Centre is staffed by fully qualified doctors, nurses and therapists; although it charges fees there are bursaries available for anyone unable to afford them.

Happiness is such an illusive element
it takes determination and love to capture it.

THE VOICE WITHIN

Inspirational poetry is the voice within, which is moulded and changed by outside influences according to one's understanding. This kind of poetry is a record, a response to a situation. It contains my observations of myself in a situation – how I feel and react – but also it is a response to what I see around me. My observations of other people and my response to their troubles and situations, and how they cope with their problems. I try to see from their point of view. The result of my observations is to respond with emotion and the voice within translates the feelings into words through poetry.

By the very act of expressing in words, thoughts and emotions, they become clarified into new meanings and understandings of human behaviour. When I explore these new meanings I find new values and form my own values in life; I develop my understanding.

I believe that the value of one's life is measured by the understanding and application of love – love from God's point of view, which is unconditional love for all things and people, whatever their race, colour or status. We have to learn to love in this way and I see our own spiritual growth as synonymous with this development.

From the voice within I try to discover more about the meaning of life and look for guidance in being a step nearer to controlling my own destiny.

I try to learn the secret of being in tune with creation, not to disturb the balance, but to live in harmony.

Words, or the lack of them, evoke all kinds of emotions – loneliness, anger, joy and unhappiness. Careless words often lead us to the wrong conclusions. Yet words are often the life-line to our sanity and become the roots of our existence.

For these reasons it is important that our words are an echo of careful thoughts and that we learn valuable lessons on life from the voice within us.

LOVE IS . . .

Love is the air that I breathe
And the mood of my being.
Love is my past
Embalmed in memories,
And my future gasping
For survival.
Love is my present
Radiant with autumn hues,
Shedding the fashioned leaves
Of myself,
Exposing the darker elements within.
Love is trusting you with the truth
Of what I am,
My soul standing naked before your eyes.
Love fashions me anew
To complement all that you are
And all that you do,
For I am no longer myself.
Love has poured me shining into your soul.

The value of a person is determined by the quality and depth of his love.

LIFE IS LIKE A RAINBOW

Life is like a rainbow tinting our emotions with every shade from elation to depression. It is the mingling of these colours that makes us what we are and controls our personal destiny.

Sometimes we find ourselves at the mercy of the age, the society, the environment or changing scene. Circumstances beyond our control change our world. At these times we have the ideal opportunity to grow beyond ourselves, to turn every disaster into a jewel, to allow us to grow in love, patience and understanding.

Sometimes we in turn are chosen to change the world for others, to provide the circumstances for others to take stock of their lives, think about the value of their lives and learn how to grow beyond themselves. Whichever side of the event we are on we feel the same emotion and absorb more of the rainbow of life. We need change to fully appreciate the intricacies of life. Disasters are temporary, but we can count our blessings forever.

WORDS

The silence of loneliness shows me naked to myself
And forces me to run away and hide
That I may not face what I am.
Not for me the rhythmic silence of contentment
When quiet thoughts replace shared conversation.
And yet so often words become the executioner
Putting to death the thoughts unfolding in my heart.
Ideas escape unripe and immature
And I am imprisoned by unthinking words.
When I treasure my silence
And explore the truth locked within my heart,
My understanding blossoms and bears fruit,
And words become meaningless
For my soul is the listener.

LOVE THE SCULPTOR

My life is measured by the progress of love.
Milestones of emotion
Declining and hurtling my soul into distraction,
Blossoming and expanding my being with sunshine.
Love can shackle, torture and condemn
The sensitive heart to a dungeon,
Where life exists in prolonged agony
Of humiliation, enslaved by monotonous routine.
But love can also set you free,
Your heart soaring in ecstasy
Of wonder and tenderness.
Anointing the eyes with the dew of beauty
To view a vital world of constant delight.

These yin-yan episodes of love
Mould us and shape the image
That we present to the world.
Each wearing a mask,
Fashioned from our experiences
And the inconstancies of love,
That bring suffering and joy
To our impressionable hearts.

HARVEST RHYTHM

As I walk the velvet hills
I look into the valley of patchwork fields;
Brown furrows, straight and stark,
Lead my eye to the fresh blossoms
In newly-painted orchards,
Wafting fragrance through the evening air.
Promises of a wealthy harvest –
Fat berries and fruits,
Clothed in warm, russet foliage,
Exhibiting brilliant hues
Before the season of rest.
Rhythms pound eternally
Throughout the seasons, year by year.
Struggle, growth and sacrifice,
Wealth and beauty, unrestricted here.
So is the pattern of our lives,
Ever-changing colour and form.
From seeds of unselfishness
Thoughts of others are born.
Nurtured with care and kindness
They will produce in time
A harvest of contentment –
The fruits of happiness.

Every moment is a gem in time, enjoy it, you will never see its sparkle again – a lost moment is a lost opportunity.

LOVE UNVEILED

Love comes in many disguises and we have to learn to recognise these. Love evokes many kinds of emotion. Sorrow, anger, joy, ecstasy are all woven into the fabric of love. Love can be fragile, yet have a great deal of strength and can pop up in the most unlikely places.

The feelings we have in the response to love, or the lack of it, are not unique, it is a human trait to respond to love. It sometimes helps to share our response by identifying with the problems and feelings of others; we may find it easier to come to terms with the pattern of our lives. Poetry about love can help us to find ourselves through understanding situations.

Love is the most important ingredient in life. It is the difference between growing and blossoming. The best specimens that blossom are those nurtured on a diet of complete love, a constant diet. For a plant only becomes sick through sudden change. We need to be aware of our responsibility to provide a constant loving environment.

In a loving environment the atmosphere vibrates and tingles in anticipation of joys to come.

LOVE UNVEILED

Love has many faces
And a vast spectrum of emotion;
You admire her radiant robe of joy
Under her cloak of desperation.

She finds man's limitations,
And clouds his mind in sorrows,
Then lifts his face to the sunshine
With dreams of rich tomorrows.

Wounds and scars are no stranger to her,
Deception and hatred her shroud,
Yet beauty and truth are her bridal gown –
She is kind, understanding, but proud.

From the heights to the depths she will lead you.
In your mind she will put out the light.
Then open the door to new wonders,
For the blind man to regain his sight.

Explore with me Pandora's box,
Let man's experiences prevail.
Feel the comforting glow of divine love,
As together Love's face we unveil.

I AM NOTHING

By myself
I am nothing –
But the rustle of leaves,
The whisper of a summer breeze,

Snowflakes falling
Aimlessly down.
Tears dripping
From bare trees.
The echoes of little waves
Lapping the shore,
And the shadow of a butterfly
On a marigold.
But now I have found You
I have become tangible,
Re-charged!
Alive!
A part of Your light.
And the world has become a beautiful place
In which to grow.

LOVE IS GIVING

Love is giving,
Love is sharing,
Love is thoughtful,
Love is caring.
Love is laughter, joy and tears,
An understanding that grows
With the years.
Love is unselfish,
Love is awareness,
Love is compassion,
Love is fairness.
Love is togetherness,
Romance for two,
Love is waiting,
For me and you.

MAGIC

I had been told about the magic.
That instant spark of confusion
Leading to ecstasy.
A mutual longing uplifting two souls
In an instant.
Outside the time and space of this world.
Magic is found in the depths
Of unselfish eyes,
Loving and caring,
Romantic and gentle.
Two souls entwining as one.
Magic must be treasured,
Defended from all intrusion,
Protected from worldly mutilation.
Nourish the magic created by destiny
And let us walk hand in hand
Into rare oblivion.

LOVE ABORTED

So alive and pure and beautiful,
Perfectly formed
And throbbing with magical breath.
Promising happiness
Stretching into eternity,
The seeds of perfection within,
Waiting to be nourished.
The living foetus
Of the poetry of life,
Delicate and fragile,
Nurturing buds of love
And unsung songs
Of happiness.

Alas! Too vulnerable,
Too perfect to blossom forth
In this harsh, unfeeling world.
Too many hazards and threats to injure
And stunt its growth.
Too perfect for this world.
Put to death in an agonising moment
Of decision.
Love incarnate,
Layed at God's feet,
To be treasured in heaven –
And here on earth becoming the ultimate sacrifice.

THE PATH TO LOVE

The silvery path to the moon
Is the path to the heart.
The silvery fingers pointing the way
To the unfolding emotion.
Reach out
And be drawn into its immeasurable robes.
Draw close
And put aside the tears of the world.
Let truth be your mantle,
Embracing your thoughts, fears and desires.
Amid the fires of dark confusion
Take shelter within your emotion;
Feel the sorrow, anguish and joy
Of affection.
One blissful moment in time to be cherished
And worn proudly like a jewel
For all eternity.

Loving unconditionally is rebirth. You become a child seeing the wonders of life for the first time and experience great joy in the creation of happiness for others.

MISSING YOU

I see your face
In the mist of my mind,
Haunting me,
Holding me.
Your smile
Caressing me,
Your voice, gentle,
Warm and tender.
The space and time
That separate us
Matter not –
For love
Overcomes all barriers,
And in our minds
We are together,
Caring, sharing, one.
And I patiently await
Your physical return,
My arms longing to embrace you,
To snuggle up –
And feel your touch;
To kiss
and drift and dream –
Without words.
Soaring together,
Joyful,
Contented,
At peace,
Complete,
– One being.

NEW LOVE

I am entranced by the new green bud
Before me.
Symbol of my summer,
Vital and bright,
Perfect in its greenness,
Bringing youth and promise,
Cloaking the secrets of tomorrow.
I ponder on its heart.
The veiled petals of perfection and fragrance
That will make it
Incomparable with all other blossom.
I am breathless with the anticipation
Of its splendour and completeness.
I am dreaming the dreams of tomorrow,
When I can bask in its radiance,
As it envelops me completely
With its aura of love;
Protecting me with strong
Yet delicate petals,
And shading me with its form
From the burning rays of society
That threaten my peace.
I have exploded
From my grinding, mechanical orbit
To grasp this cherished bud.
It will bloom for me
And I in turn will blossom,
Warmed by its care.
Welcome Love!

UNDER YOUR SPELL

The way that you smile,
Radiating love;
In your silence reaching out
To my uncertainty.
Your beckoning aura, magnetic,
Draws me near
For the shadow of your love
To engulf me.
Your eyes, ever changing,
Revealing all,
Imparting knowledge soundlessly,
Empowered with a strange compulsion
Which draws forth my soul.
Master of my heart
And my whole metabolism,
Which changes at your command,
Draining my emotion,
Engulfing my life,
Drawing me onwards until we are one.
I have become
The breadth of your aura.
Most willingly I come,
Drawn by the very nature of you,
Compressed in the shining light
That radiates from your soul.

SHARING LOVE

Can you share my love
With the unloved of this world,
Souls reaching out in torment,
So tired and lost and hurt?

Can you share in my compassion
As through this tortured world we walk,
Giving tender understanding
To the ones who need it most?

My path has been dismal and thorny,
I understand sorrow and pain,
But God gave me love in abundance,
To rise beyond suffering, unchanged.

The knowledge of love I store in my heart,
The frailty of man I know well,
But all people in need are God's children
And I must help them whenever I can.

I have wanted so much to be cared for,
To have a true love of my own,
To hold me, to know me, to love me,
To share in the world that I know.

My dreams were but dreams 'til I found you,
In the light of your love I now grow,
Every moment that we are together
Our love will grow stronger, I know.

We are to each other a mirror
Reflecting the light of true love,
In strength we will shine in the darkness
And share with the world what we have.

In a tormented world of destruction
We found beauty beyond all our dreams.
The beauty of knowing each other,
And the wonder true happiness brings.

ROMANTIC INTERLUDE

My heart is in the Hebrides,
Lost in time,
Sitting with my love
On black rocks streaked with yellow lichen.
In a lonely, sun-baked bay we sat,
Unaware of anything
But the warmth and closeness
And the magic of togetherness,
When time stood still
And the world melted away.
The sun shone brightly on our love
As we sat in silent embrace,
Serenaded by the lapping waves
Dancing on the white, gleaming sand.
Water filled upturned shells,
Captured the sun
And sparkled like diamonds.
Spring-green water splayed out
In gentle circles
In that Utopian bay,
Where love reigned supreme.
We walked slowly hand in hand
Amid the bleached, fluted shells,
Drinking in the hot sun.
Lost in our own happiness
We watched the bright, green seaweed swaying
As unforgettable memories
Were ripe in the throes of creation.

RELATIONSHIPS

All through our lives people's paths cross and recross with each other. Often with our limited human mind we do not understand the significance of our meetings. Yet every experience we encounter adds something to our lives and penetrates one or more of our varied emotions. This gives us additional knowledge of ourselves, each other and the world.

The collector and contemplater of these experiences not only grows in wisdom and understanding, but is able to become a valuable contributor. It is then possible to anticipate needs and add value to the lives of others by a positive response.

We do not always understand our own path or our meaning on the path of another. Only a higher being is able to reveal such truths. However, all relationships, however short, and whatever they offer us, should be treasured, for in some way they will give us the chance to grow and love unconditionally.

Explore love in all its facets and discover its enduring brilliance.

THIS MAN THAT I LOVE

This man that I love
Uplifts me with his laughter,
Breathing inspiration into an empty day.
His imagination creates a fantasy
In a humdrum world of monotony
So loved by our society.
A world of dubious values,
Empty of meaning.

This man that I love
Is the clown on the hill,
Aware of the lonely people all around.
Hiding his own sorrow with laughter
And confusing everyone
With his chameleon nature.
Restless, he drives himself
Until he is too tired to think –
Or reminisce . . . . .

Yet he is warm, considerate
And full of romantic dreams
Which mould his life,
Creating moments of rare ecstasy
When they escape and flow towards me.
A rare man,
A magnificent man.
Unreachable in his self-made fortress . . .

But, I love him.

GOOD FRIENDS

No words can express
How I feel
About my friends.
Togetherness cries out
In the silence
Of our greeting.
And the interlude
Between our meetings
Is a timeless fraction of our lives
For we are never apart.
A touch is worth a thousand words
For it expresses the comfort and concern
That radiates from your souls.
Give not to me,
But to those lost souls in need.
For I am but another island,
A sanctuary in the troubled sea of life.
Nourished by God's light
We three are one.
We know that sometimes clouds
Must cross the face of the sun,
That we may know ourselves –
A tiny grain of wheat
Empty of His light,
Helpless.
Only with His light can we grow strong
To nourish others.
This knowledge binds us together
As we struggle
To keep on the path of humility
And our souls are forever
Locked in an embrace.

TEACHER RETIRING

Will they ever know
How much I really cared?
How I listened for each falling sound
As their minds acknowledged words
And understanding dawned?

Will they ever know
How hard I tried
To give them respect for each other
And each natural miracle
Taking place
In the world around them?

Will they ever know
How much I worried
About their values
And the ways they made their mark
Upon the unfolding world
That engulfed them?

Will they ever know
All the things I planned
For each one to blossom,
To grow in understanding
And expand in knowledge?

All the hundreds of young lives
That have tugged at my heart strings
With their individual problems;
Tried my patience
With their antics
And depended on my praise
Rewarding their efforts.

Now, tired and drained,
Sapped of energy
And in pain,
Still I love and still I care –
Not willingly retreating
Or abandoning their cause –
But will they ever know?

A NEW ERA

You were written into my soul
At the beginning of time,
Beyond the understanding
Of the physical here and now,
But in an ageless emotion of unity.
Together we will conquer convention
And all the patterns of behaviour
Designed by our self-orientated society.
For we are two people with one soul,
Fired, inspired and radiating
Oneness of thought and realisation
Of all that the world has lost
Through its preoccupation
With shallow pursuits into the realm
Of instant pleasure.
For our desires are deep rooted
In the humanity of each other.
And our love has a burnished glow,
Polished by the cloth of time,
Patience and unselfishness.
It sparkles with the promise of tomorrow.

It's the little things in life that matter; thoughtfulness that makes each day special for the one in your care.

UNCONDITIONAL LOVE

How can I quench the thirst of longing to be with you?
Or satisfy the hunger to be at your side,
The gnawing pain of despair that separation brings?
Or comfort my shivering soul
Crying out for your warmth?
I am a spirit without an age in which to dwell,
Unable to conform to man's inhumanity to man;
Unable to wear the cloak of love
As a fashion for the here and now,
Casting it aside on a personal whim.
Time has taught me to seek nothing
And expect only the fickleness of man's desires,
Experiencing his changing emotion as I do the seasons.
Life has taught me how to love unconditionally,
Preparing me for you.
In one fleeting instant of meeting
I had loved you timelessly
For all eternity.
I have welcomed pain and sorrow,
For the depth of my pain is also
The depth of my joy.
The pangs of longing that I feel
Are the depths of my desire to give,
Care, and understand you,
Devoting my life to loving you.
I offer all that I am –
My feelings, thoughts, words and life.
And although I need your love so much,
I shall ask nothing –
Except that I may love you
And that we may look at life together sometimes,
Through shared eyes.

S. O. S.

I found myself standing
In still waters at the sea's edge,
As if manacled by the shifting sand
Beneath my toes.
I looked out at the horizon
At the huge tidal wave,
Growing with terrible force,
Rolling relentlessly towards me.
I stood transfixed
Like a rabbit frozen in the headlights,
Hypnotised, unable to retreat;
Waiting to be engulfed
By forbidden desires.
It crashed over me
Breaking in whirlfoams
Of terrible ecstasy.

LAMENT OF A TENNIS WIDOW or I WANDERED LONELY . . . BECAUSE OF TENNIS

They rose up soaring to the sky,
Tossed up on high o'er men so tall,
Then all at once he heaved a sigh
To see the golden tennis ball,
Beside the net, beneath the trees,
Bouncing and rolling in the breeze.

Continuous as the stars that shine
And twinkle on the tennis court,
It bounced on never-ending lines
Towards the net, but stopping short.
Ten thousand curses floated by,
His partner shook his head and sighed.

The trees beside it swayed, but it
Out-did the graceful trees in glee.
The poet in amazement sits
Watching the leaping company.
I gazed and gazed – but little thought
What wealth to me the sport had brought!

For oft when on my couch I lie,
Thinking the game must be a joke,
Those figures flash before my eye
And racquets swing in cherished strokes.
The net, the veil of the poet's pall,
Dances beneath that wretched ball.

THE MOST PRECIOUS THINGS IN LIFE

The shimmering moon caressing the sea,
The evening sun setting fire to the sky,
The sparkling waters that leap down the rocks
And the rustling trees that talk to the wind.
These precious gifts to all men are free
But belong to those who know how to see.
Men who desire wealth, power and fame
Live in a gilded cage.
They offer a woman material things –
Buying gold-plated happiness
That will tarnish with the passing of time.
Offer me understanding and hope,
A sharing of troubles and joys,
Romance and deep affection
And comfort in times of stress.
We can explore life together
With laughter and tears of joy
And treasure the precious things in life
That wealth is unable to buy.

GIVE AND TAKE

How was your day, my darling?
Tell me – I want to share.
I want to know how you have coped
Because I care . . .
Tell me about your problems –
What happened at work today.
I may not fully understand
But I'll comment – if I may.

What made you laugh,
What made you sad,
What difficulties overcome?
Are you disheartened?
Or hopeful still –
I'm glad that you've come home.

How are your friends?
How well did you play?
Tell me the latest jokes.
What are your plans ?
When will you meet?
What are your future hopes?

I see you are tired now,
Energy spent.
You have no more to say.
Your thoughts, your feelings,
Your daily life,
Are locked in my heart today . . .
Because I love,
Because I care –
All that you do,
I want to share.

UNHAPPINESS

Happiness makes living easier, but unhappiness gives us a chance to grow beyond ourselves.

There are many causes of unhappiness, both external and internal. Whatever the cause, it is how we deal with our sorrow that really matters.

The first step to take is to admit to ourselves that we are unhappy and then to accept our state of mind and isolate the cause. Once we have admitted and accepted the cause of our unhappiness we are then in a position to begin to deal with it and change it. We want to change it, to progress, to grow in spirit.

Strange as it may seem, unhappiness is a great gift in our lives as it is the ideal ingredient for spiritual growth, it is food for the soul.

NEGLECTED HEART

Here I am,
The whisper of yesterday,
The echo of then, not now –
Or what is to be.
My life energy momentarily still,
Numb in my silence.
I am but a shadow of myself
Caught up in the emotion of the present.
My sensitivity stifles me
And my spirit is frozen
By the feeling of rejection.
I fight invisible fiends
That prey on my soul
And I am helpless,
Questioning the value of my life.
And I drift in a coma state
Waiting for love.

EQUINE SPIRIT

I pound my hooves with the anger of my longing,
I toss my mane with the fury of desire.
My heart beats out a lonely rhythm
That bursts into my ears
Making me cry out in desperation
For your love.
I shy from the terrors of reality,
Prancing nervously –
Poised for flight;

Running in circles
From the aching of my feelings,
Wanting to come to you
For affection and love –
To feel your hand calming,
Reassuring,
Banishing my tears of despair,
Telling my trembling body
To be at peace,
Because you care for me.

A BLADE OF GRASS

Life is like a well-kept lawn
And I a blade of grass
Struggling constantly towards the light,
Trying to grow tall.
Pushed and jostled by stronger neighbours,
Trodden on and crushed –
By feet, paws and objects.
Just when I feel vital and strong
I am cut down,
To begin my struggle again,
Feeling weak and parched
In the hot sun.
I know if this lawn became neglected
I would be stifled and imprisoned
In airless darkness
By my strong, dominant fellows
Reaching for the light.
I would wither and die unnoticed.
Why is life such a struggle?

Make every day a kaleidoscope of light through loving thoughts.

LEARNING TO LOVE

Where is love hiding in our city streets?
The alleys echo silent shrieks
Of violent deeds
That man perpetrates against his own kind.
The scowling adolescent
Venting his uncontrolled aggression
On an elderly innocent,
To secure material gain or some distorted emotion
Only he can acknowledge as pleasure.
Children, innocent and vulnerable,
Play in ungodly places,
Open and loving in an unloved air
Destined to echo with their screams of anguish.
Where is love hiding in the daily headlines
Shouting horror from the written page
As it crawls boldly into our early morning homes?
Mankind is still an infant,
Uncontrolled in his desires,
Self-centred in his tantrums,
Unthinking in his values.
Yet in man's nature is a spark of love
Waiting to be ignited and guided.
One loving soul is like the courageous flower
That blooms in a forgotten corner of a derelict dump.
Love is infectious and can melt the hardest heart,
A candle shining in the darkest night.
A seed of love is the hope of tomorrow,
The beginning of the garden we desire to see.
When learning to love we explore understanding,
And from these roots forgiveness flows.

Loving the unloving is the hardest bridge to cross;
But success restores the balance in these souls that God had lost.

WHO CARES?

The land is littered with the crippled remains
Of the people.
The broken spirits and mangled emotions
Of the deserted.
As the battle cry of 'LOVE!' echoes through the hills,
And the sword of deception
Descends with noisy clatter
Upon the shield of innocence,
Cutting it in two.
But who cares?

When the physical remnants of brave men
Lay like garbage, forgotten, in the trenches long ago,
Righteous men cried out in anguish
To stir the humanity in men's hearts,
To raise them up in angry outcry,
To pierce the conscience of society
And demand an end to the slaughter.
And some cared!

Now, all around is the camouflaged battlefield,
Stained with anguished tears of the lonely and unloved.
This war is accepted, expected, almost a joke.
Lust and desire are the fashion of the day.
Responsibility outdated. 'We must change with the times!'
'All's fair in love and war!'
'You win some, you lose some!'
And laughter stifles the anguished sighs
And hopeless emptiness.
But who cares?

'It's one of those things!' they say.
'She nags!' 'He's boring!'
'I don't want him anymore!'
'I don't love her!'

And so the selfish assault continues
Under the guise of so-called love.
'I love another!' shoots from the bow of desire
Piercing countless victims,
Leaving them numb,
Motionless, bewildered.
And their mechanical bodies
Grind on through their daily routine.
As their love is ground to dust,
As ashes to ashes –
But who cares?
And the true banner of love,
Made from self-sacrifice and understanding,
Concern for the true happiness
Of the partner,
Has long lain torn, trampled and forgotten
In the sludge of inhumanity
That has become the fertile bed
That breeds our society.
They who bravely ride into battle,
Hacking hearts to pieces
In the name of love;
Leaving a trail of devastated beings
Weeping to unlistening ears.

And I cry with shame
That I was born of this species,
And my heart reaches out with compassion
To the injured souls –
For I care!

OASIS IN REJECTION

A moment of togetherness
Captured in bewilderment.
Hearts reaching out for comfort,
Knowing they will find understanding
In a rare friendship.
And in troubled times
Our souls glanced at each other
And entwined –
In drifting dreams,
Sheltering each other
From stormy seas of emotion
And chaos.
And escaping from the world
We held each other
And cared.

Now those precious moments
Have become memories
To be cherished.
Yet, I wonder if you are wishing
The memory away.
Or whether the drifting dream
Passed so quickly
That it slipped by unnoticed,
Without meaning –
Never to become
A memory in your heart.

My heart ached
When I saw your unhappiness,
And I wanted to reach out
In compassion
And comfort you.
But our souls reached out together –
And I am left with a bewildered heart
And shaken emotions
Because I did not know
How much I really cared –
For you!

REACH OUT FOR ME

Reach out for me, I am here.
My heart is waiting,
Crying out for affection.
I reach for your hand
But you remain deep in your silent thoughts,
Ignorant of my presence.
With all my being I shower you with care
To remind you of my feelings.
Why do you never reach for me?
Love, romance, affection
Are inseparable in my soul.
I thirst for all three.
When I find them lacking I become disorientated,
Unsure of my place in life.
I question my existence and feel insecure.
If you really care that I am a part of your life,
Show me, touch me, tell me –
Reach out for me!

THE MAN IN THE PARK

The old man sits on a bench in the park,
Staring at the asphalt
Framed between his ancient toes.
His faded hat pulled low over his brow
Shuts out the crowd of crocuses
Reaching for attention beside him.
Motionless he sits,
Oblivious of the noisy lorries thundering
Along the busy street behind him.
His dark, time-worn clothes
Hang loosely on his shrunken form,
A reminder of a more robust past
Before the leaner years became his reality.
He sits transfixed,
Staring at the ground,
Fascinated by a vision
Unseen by lesser eyes as ours.
A bold robin approaches,
Hungry for new perches
On this statue that merges so well
Into the shadows of the nearby trees.

A sigh ripples through the man
Slumped on the park bench.
His gnarled, bent fingers quiver
Like the last ripple in a disturbed pond,
But his gaze never falters.
Cut off from the sights and sounds,
The movement and the fragrance
Of his bustling environment,
He is locked in timeless wanderings within –
He is alone!

HOPE

When the cloak of loneliness enfolds me
And the robe of rejection drapes my form;
When unkind words are a crown for my head
And deception binds my weary feet –
Then the silence of a loveless world
Deafens me.
And the sunlight of selfishness
Blinds me.
I feel my life blood drifting away,
And my spirit knows famine and drought.
Numbed of emotion,
I fade unnourished.
And in that instant
I feel Your pain so deeply.
The thorns of mockery,
Your love rejected,
The weight of Your cross,
Your wounds, Your misery –
But most of all I feel
The loneliness
Of Your crucifixion,
And I understand.
Suddenly I realise
That HOPE
Is all the nourishment I need.
You have given me hope and strength
To give Your selfless love.
And when I finally leave this place,
No trace of me you'll find –
Except in men's hearts,
For they will know
I loved – I cared!

SPIRITUAL GROWTH

We need strength to take charge of our lives and deal with the situations that offer us spiritual growth. To become unselfish, to learn self-sacrifice and to accept and make positive the many difficult times in our lives when we feel that 'fate' has been a little 'unfair'.

We need something to give us strength. This is found in divine love. Spiritual love is a divine understanding on a give and take basis. We need to take from divine love to make us strong within, to deal with whatever comes along, whether it is our own or other people's problems. We have to learn to take from God's love as well as give in return for the joy of being alive and in the position to put meaning into our lives.

Spiritual growth takes place when you learn to love other people beyond the boundaries of your own needs and desires. This is a task for life and can only be achieved by drawing on divine strength and remaining ever aware of the need to put yourself in second place.

SPIRITUAL STRENGTH

Without you it is winter.
My day is crammed with empty routine,
Actions rattling coldly in a vacuum.
Days drifting by, namelessly,
Starved of any emotion
To germinate the seeds
That perpetuate beautiful memories.
My hibernating heart lies suspended,
Held inactive
By the clinical environment
That anaesthetises my being.
Time floats by on bronze leaves
That leap from the chestnut tree
Outside my window.
She is wearing a carpet of welcome
For your arrival.
I am waiting patiently,
Remote from the dissection and removal
Of my fleshy walls.
Waiting for your kiss
To release me from my coma
So that I might understand
The meaning of my life,
And accept the challenge
To overcome all that threatens
The progress of my soul.
Within me a light is ready
To ignite and shine out
Beyond all boundaries
And limitations that my body
Has chosen to create.
I will overcome all obstacles

To free my spirit,
To express my love
And share what I have learned –
God give me strength!

PRAYER

Many pray in distress or need
When their heart is full of sorrow.
Harvest your joy –
Pray when your heart is full of gladness.
Prayer is an expansion of yourself,
Pouring your life force into the living ether.
Radiate the shining light of joy from your heart
To brighten the darkness that flows from you
When you seek comfort.
Come with laughter not tears to the Oneness.
Prepare yourself to meet all those
Who at that time offer up prayer
And move towards the light –
For you may never touch that soul again.
Do not enter the temple of light
With requests for yourself or others –
But remain invisible, unheard.
Approach in ecstasy.
It is enough that you have come with joy
Into the presence of the Father.
For He knows your needs and desires now,
Even before you were born.
And He knows the ways of your heart.
Come not dressed in words or thoughts,
But only the desire to harmonise
And be at One.

SEEDS OF LOVE

The many seeds of love
Lie dormant in my soul,
Waiting for the nourishment
To make them grow;
Waiting for waves of compassion in me
To stir them into life,
And unselfish care of others
To unfurl them and grow strong.
Love's garden flourishes within
In every shape and form,
Sending out a fragrance
That envelops everyone.
Your love inspires your children
To grow in thought and care,
Your partner sees that life is good
And shares the ups and downs.
Yet all those who breathe
This earthly air
With joy, or pain, or sorrow,
Will grow beyond their bonds of self
Through love.
They give hope for tomorrow.

THE WATERS OF LIFE

I stand by the lake shore,
Feet rooted in the Waters of Life
That pulse through Your veins,
Bathed in the warm glow
That radiates from Your face
When You look on me.
I am overwhelmed by Your love
That enfolds me tightly,

Carrying me away from myself
And all that I have been.
You swept me up into Your love
In an instant of ecstatic joy,
Engulfing me.
And I was bathed in the light
Of paradise and reborn.
And in those moments of oblivion
The Waters of Life
Flowed through the famined earth.
And You entered creation
In brilliant splendour
Through the glory of Your sacrifice.
And the life blood flowed
To replenish the land,
Dispersing through the waters
And lapping at my feet,
Nourishing the need of love within me.
And silent overtures of hope
Arose from the lake,
Filling the purified air
With the music of Your presence.
And I was held enraptured,
Overwhelmed by the beauty of Your love.
And I turned to the woods
And the hills and the sky;
They were alive with Your presence,
Touched by the sign of Your brightness,
For now redemption irrigates our land.

A NEW BEGINNING

I welcome each new dawn.
I hover on vibrating wings.
I soar upwards into Your light
And my heart sings.
My spirit is unchained,
Freed from the shackles of mortal need,
No longer resisting,
Beyond self desires and human greed.
I no longer strive for earthly love,
My pliable being I offer to You.
Instruct me in self-sacrifice,
Teach me new ways Your work to do.
Share with me the secrets
Of Your all-embracing heart.
Show me the way to truly love,
Teach me the right way to start.
I want to remain beyond myself
To retain Your inspiring breath within,
To carry Your love to Your children.
Lord, show me the right way to begin.

Without love I am lost and grope like a blind man in a forest of thorns.

GIVING

You collect about you material things
For fear you will need them tomorrow.
But that fear is a need in itself
That can never be satisfied.
When your larder is full
Your fear of hunger will still be with you
As you strive to keep it full.
When you give away your material goods
You give little.
Only when you give of yourself –
Your strength, your thoughts, your understanding –
Do you truly give.
If you give a little of your many possessions,
With the desire for gratitude or recognition,
Then the gift is worthless.
If you have little and give all that you have, gladly,
Then your gift is priceless.
The believers in life are rich in life,
And set no value on material things,
And need nothing, except to know that they are alive.

Give with joy and you are repaid with joy,
Give with pain and you receive pain.
Give with understanding,
Unasked, unannounced, where you see need,
And expect no reward,
And the Father will shine through you,
Guiding your heart and your actions;
Seeing through your eyes
And smiling on His children.

The giver is the place
Where the Father reaches out
To comfort His child.
Know this and be worthy of giving.
Let awareness of self dissolve into the earth
And give invisibly.

BEHOLD MY MASTER

Father, I come into Your presence
As each day dawns.
I bow down before You,
Awed by the ever-changing
Ceremonial robes
That You wear to greet me;
Moved by the kaleidoscope of colours
And intricate shapes
Woven into Your rustling, swirling garments
Displayed before me.
My appreciating heart is filled
With Your splendour,
And I feel Your greatness
Enveloping the shadow that is me.
I feel Your gentle tenderness
As I stand before You,
I, so small and insignificant
And unworthy of Your care.
I desire to serve You,
To walk in the shade of Your splendour;
To touch Your heaven-spun robes,
To marvel at their beauty;
But most of all
To share in the love in Your heart.

UNRIVALLED TREASURE

I met Him on the curved shore
Of Scarista bay
And he showed me all the treasures
That He had created.
The emerald-sapphire blend
Of clear, sparkling water
Edged in snow-white gossamer,
Restless explosions of gleaming foam.
And He drew his regal mantle
Around the sparkling, shell-crushed sand,
Smooth and pure, stretching towards
The green-topped dunes.
On the shore He lay before my feet
A carpet of multi-coloured shells
Of every shade and hue,
Reflecting nature's colours
Throughout all creation;
Displaying her changing mood
And restless nature
In bands of brilliance
On delicate, restful shades
Captured in the fragile cusps
Of the jewel shells studding
That silent, desolate shore.
Shy islands, purple crowned,
Cloaked in green and brown,
Rise up in splendour from the sea.
Sharp, dark rocks, shining,
Clothed in foam,
Beckon with craggy fingers
From the corner of the bay.
Toe Head rises dramatically,
Commanding respect from the bejewelled bay
Which sways gently in rhythmic obedience
At His regal feet.

All this He sets before me.
Intoxicating beauty that fills my senses,
And stimulating, perfumed air
That fills my lungs.
I am lightheaded with the joy that penetrates my being
And I stand on the shore, overawed,
Feeling so small and humble,
Less significant than the tiniest grain
Beneath my feet.
I am filled with the glory of being alive
And a witness to such splendour.
As I absorb it with childish delight,
My tears of emotion
Go out to my Creator
As my spirit ascends,
Crying out expression
In unison with the lonely seagull cry.

Isle of Harris

DESPAIR

Despair is a feeling known to everyone. It causes an inner numbness which clouds our reasoning so that we find it difficult to be rational and make decisions that will lead us onto firmer footing. Often despair is caused by other people's treatment of us and we temporarily lose the strength, and sometimes the will, to improve our situation. We have to force ourselves into the reality of value in our environment and minimise the hurt to ourselves.

What really matters in life is that flowers continue to bloom, birds sing and the seasons change, making a beautiful environment for those who are really able to see its value.

Despite the destructive nature of man and his ability to create havoc – there *is* hope. Man can conjure up an atmosphere of hate, wrought from his own self-centred ego, rife with malice. Yet true, honest values are never destroyed, no matter how powerful an enemy is as he creates gloom for you.

Love is indestructible. It is a spiritual state to love the natural world and all people in it. The body may become frail, sick and vulnerable, but the inner self is strong. In times of stress, cruel words and actions, the inner self increases in determination that love will bring spiritual peace.

RESTLESSNESS

So grow the seeds of doubt
And indecision;
The restless sense of wondering
On flowers unpicked
And fields unmown;
Perusing beauties
Unadmired,
And harvests unsown.

The world is your oyster
But will you find the pearl?
Thoughts are the seeds
Of action –
To realise our dreams,
To explore our hopes,
To search, and attain our desires
And seek fulfilment
As we walk in new pastures.

You walk in the new, fragrant meadow
Intoxicated, rapturous,
Immersed in the wonder of new love.
Shaking off your memories
You are reborn.
Convinced that the sweet meadow
Will be everlasting fresh,
And autumn will not come,
When colours fade
And fragrance goes,
And the meadow lies sterile
Beneath a mantle of leaves –
Cast-off hopes.

Now where can you roam,
Unsheltered, unfed, unloved?
You return to your crops,
Your field that sustained you
And nurtured and grew for you –
But it is choked with weeds
There is famine in the land.

CONFESSION

When I was young I filled my life
With things I liked to do.
There was no time to sit and talk,
There was no time to share.
There was little time to visit friends,
There was no time to really care.
Every hour of every week
Was filled with work or play;
With a family to attend to
There was no time to pray!
And so I wove those fragile threads
Until my life's cloth was illusion;
And I grew old within its web
Until it acted as a mirror.
It reflected bright my selfishness,
My greed and lack of care;
My friends, my work, my health were gone,
I had lost the road to prayer.
I had not spared a moment to love my fellow man,
Time was illspent on idle tasks,
Now I have to live with who I am!

Spring clean your inner self. Frank honesty prevents the web of misunderstanding being woven in dark corners.

SPIDER'S WEB

Suspended feelings,
Anaesthetised.
Drifting mind
Held in the vice
Of numbness
Created by the little, blue pills –
Forcing forgetfulness
And masking
The joy-pain sorrow
Of a love-torn mind –
Until the effects wear off!

Better to run away
And escape physically
From the anguish of the present
And the future.
Escape from untold hurts
And rejection.
Feelings unconsidered,
Ignored, abused;
Emotions trampled,
And the selfishness
That acts as executioner!
And the 'cat' loses one more life!

But maybe it's better
To destroy oneself.
To commit emotional suicide
So that there is no longer
A heart that feels emotion,
And love is destroyed for ever.
And the physical zombie will continue
On its mechanical way,
Concerned with humdrum routine,
And no longer able to reach out,

Or feel, or share
The joyful pain of love's illusion.
No longer fall victim
To the needs or hungers of men.
Or be tempted by the fantasy
Of love's promise,
That changes from a dream
To a nightmare
Of pain and anguish
That shatters my soul.

This is surely the answer.
Destruction of feeling.
Unable to respond,
Or become a part
Of what masquerades as love.
I must become uncaring,
Unattached;
Destroy myself
Before I am destroyed
By uncaring selfishness
That seeks my heart
And saps my strength
And tosses me aside
When all is spent.
And I become the sacrifice
For the spider.

STRUGGLE

In my loneliness have I found You.
I have seen You shining
In the darkness of my soul
And felt You near
As I stumbled, haltingly,

In the shadow of myself.
In the silence of my sorrow
I heard Your voice calling faintly,
Like a mystic echo
In my deaf ears.
As I groped blindly
Through the haze of my mind,
The thought of You was there,
Like an island shining
In a restless sea.
And as I withdrew
Into my self-made chrysalis
Of safety –
Fleeing from the terrors
Of this cruel world's deception –
I found You there.
And You warmed my shivering self-centredness
Until it melted away.
I stepped into Your Light,
Holding out my hand
For reassurance.
You removed my cloak of despair
And gave me hope.

I no longer dwell in the shadows
Of a life suppressed
Or linger on the precipice
Of despair.
I have lost all self-awareness,
Now I live in You –
As a part of that shining Light
That loves
And uplifts
The hearts of men.

THE TANGLED MIND OF A MENTALLY DISTURBED WOMAN

I see you
But are you really there?
I hear your voice,
But it's so far away.
Meaningless words
Bombard my ears.
I peer into the shadows
And strange, black shapes
Jump out and mock me.
The Light has gone out of my world,
And I grope in the haze
Of the extinguished candle,
As I stumble in the maze
Of my mind.
I seek only a familiar thing or place,
That I may know that I am,
And not a dream of myself
Floating timelessly in space.
Faces pass by, grey and expressionless,
Turning away from me.
I have lost my Lord
And all is darkness.
In my unreal world
I seek a memory to anchor my mind.
I play the records
That once nourished my soul,
For 'Music is a glimpse into the infinite' –
I need you now, Lord!
But the music sounds out
Harsh and meaningless,
And I flounder helplessly
In the whirlpool of my mind.
Help me, Lord!
I see a spark of Your light

In the eyes of a stranger,
I reach out and grasp her hand.
I struggle to emerge from my cocoon
Like an overdue butterfly.
I feel your warmth and comfort, Lord,
And I now know that You cannot come to me.
I must seek You out.
Your dwelling place is in the hearts
Of those that love others.
Let me hold you tight, stranger,
For I fear I slip away into another dream.
Let me see You, Lord,
Shining from her eyes,
That I may know You care
That I am alive!
Am I alive?
I look into her eyes
And see – not a stranger
But a replica of myself
Looking back.
And I know that You are here, Lord!

BUTTERFLY

I am a butterfly
Alighting on your hand.
Your fingers close around me.
Incarcerated in a warm womb of flesh,
With quivering wings
I stand transfixed
In the stifling darkness.
And the dust of my colours
Penetrates your palm,
Absorbed into your flesh.

Suddenly my prison springs open,
Exposing me to the sunshine.
But the moment of awareness is now my past,
I cannot fly away.
The vibrance of flight has gone.
The pattern of my wings is imprinted
On your spirit forever.

Will you place me on a nearby flower
In the hope that I will fly away –
And not consider the thought
That I may fade and die?
Or will you carry me with you?
Your butterfly
Will not flutter by!

MORNING LIGHT, LAKE CONISTON

The silence sings loudly in my ears
And the warm sun pierces my flesh.
The rushing beck pulses through my veins
And the lapping lake ripples through my head.
My mind, tense with the problems of yesterday,
Defends the shadows of myself,
The tortured spirit striving to survive
In the desert of man's inhumanity.
Caution, my veil, shrouds me,
And I want to walk invisibly,
Even in this place.
Yet nature enfolds me in her green mantle
And I am comforted.
The tension dissolves
As I cast off my armour of despair
And bask naked in the sunshine of Your presence.
I feel the seeds of hope planted in this ground,
Growing strongly into tomorrow's dream –
When man will love man
Selflessly,
Causing their souls to sparkle
And fuse into Your divine light.
As I walk in this garden,
Let me cast off the shackles and chains
That bind me to my dark, imprisoned self,
And as a free spirit reach out to others –
An invisible channel of Your love,
And with my true family
Embrace peace.

PERSONAL EFFORT

There are many meaningless activities in people's lives and only too often these come so much to the fore that there is no time left for really important things. If we only stopped once in a while and thought clearly about our lives and the true meaning of our existence. If we pondered on our achievements in relation to the rest of the world and other people, then there would be many changes and life would take on new values.

Love is the most precious emotion given to man, but often its value is lost, or it is abused or neglected. To experience the highest form of love we must treasure it in all its aspects and keep it in full bloom by constant attention and nourishment, by making it a lifetime's work.

LOVE IS FRAGILE

Love is like a wild flower,
Beautiful and delicate.
Driven by a mystic force
It grows and blossoms,
Raising its delicate frame
In unlikely places;
Appearing like magic
Among the rubble of mankind;
Battling through concrete
And walls
To perfume the air –
And to please the eyes
Of the beholder
Who stumbles on this miracle
And wonders at its strength.

The fragrant, stubborn survivor
That blossoms,
Rooted in determination,
Battered and tossed by the elements,
In a forgotten corner
Of a hostile environment
Created by Man.
No sign of nourishment or care,
Yet the solitary flower
Emerges
From the concrete chrysalis,
Unfolding its delicate wings,
And stretches up,
Searching for the sun,
Swaying in the breeze,
Unnoticed –
Ignored –
Unannounced;
Abused by nameless feet,

Unseen by sightless eyes,
Waiting for the one
Who sees with his heart
And wonders at the miracle
Waiting – just for him
To capture the beautiful wildness
And cherish its magical strength,
While it blooms – for him,
Carrying the secret
Of perpetual life.

But –
Love is like a wild flower.
Left in its dark corner,
Ignored, unnourished,
It fades and withers,
Vanishes without trace,
The life force crushed.
Love is like a wild flower –
FRAGILE!

When you wonder whether you can spare the time to visit someone to listen, to talk and to share, remember that it is a two-way experience. You both have a great deal to offer towards each other's spiritual growth.

MAN IS A THIEF

Man is a thief,
A magpie, collecting to appease
His own desires.
Stealing the love from his children
As he deserts his young family
To follow his own selfish pursuits;
Stealing the love from his wife
To lavish on another,
To pay for new favours
That give him comfort and pleasure.
Sometimes a mother is a thief,
Stealing time from the needs
Of her growing family,
Relinquishing her role of guide,
Teacher and comforter –
In order to work for her own pleasure;
Easing her conscience with material gifts –
Buying herself out of her maternal role.
We steal divine love in our eloquent way,
Leading others away from God;
Talking away his existence and works,
Robbing Him of our response
To the gifts of creation.
Time, Duty, Love, Responsibility and Prayer –
All these we steal,
Observed by each other.
We are rarely condemned, punished
Or cast away.
Our actions are familiar, condoned,
Even applauded.
Yet – if man steals one material thing
He is condemned, punished and humiliated.
For things take precedence over feelings.
The finality of the horror
Evoked by his actions

Leaves no room for forgiveness.
Every man sits in judgement
On his fellow man,
Extending the punishment with gossip
By his own abhorrence
Of this one particular theft
Which has no place in his life.
And in his arrogance
He commits the greatest theft of all.
He steals the divine authority
To sit in judgement over another soul –
When his own heart is filled
With the spoils of a lifetime,
Hidden in the shadows of his deeds.

THINK TWO

Two can share,
One can be selfish.
Two can be thoughtful
And care for each other.
One can be self-centred.
Two can comfort when things go wrong.
One can be sad, alone.
Two can be companions –
One can be lonely.
Two can be loyal and give support,
One can feel rejected and insecure.
Two can fulfil the meaning of love,
One can never be complete.
If there is no one to receive
All is lost in love and care
For this is a two-person world to share.

The code by which you live sharpens your actions and your behaviour. Your understanding, opinions and values shape your personality.

TO BE LOVED

When you are loved –
When you know affection,
Care and understanding,
And feel the joy of needs fulfilled;
When arms reach out to comfort you,
And your world is seen
Through another's eyes –
Be thankful,
And channel that love
To those less fortunate than you.
Those unloved souls
Who struggle on
In timeless loneliness.
And if you feel that you are unloved,
Uncomforted, unheard,
Then rise up like an unnourished flower
And seek the Light.
Grow strong in the warmth of His care.
Step beyond yourself,
And let your hollow being
Channel that divine love
That it may flow to others –
Unselected, all embracing.
And be thankful that you are giving.

Desire nothing for yourself,
And pray –
Not that you might be loved
But that you may go on loving
Endlessly,
For you are the spark
And hope
Of times to come;
And the beginning
Of the promised land.

THE OBSERVER

Hiding among the shadows of life,
I peer out and watch the peacocks
Strutting in the sunshine,
So proud and bold,
Knowing themselves and sharing
Their confidence with the world.
I fade into the shadow of the wall,
Clinging tight like the ivy,
Passing unnoticed, unchanging,
Firmly rooted upon my path.
I quietly sit observing
The metamorphosis of society –
Girls preening in their
Multicoloured beauty
That fades so soon,
Mocking the world.
Grey shapes move down well-worn tracks,
Eating up the routine of their lives
In manual labour.
Obliterating the line between life and work,
Deaf to the voice within,
Humanity rushes onwards
In a tidal wave of diversions
And indecisions.
Butterflies of every hue and size,
Dazzled by the petals of the shops,
Flit aimlessly
Collecting bright treasures.

GROW YOUR OWN LOVE

New love is a fantasy,
An illusion that numbs our senses
And cuts us off from the reality of the world –
Those unseen faces watching from behind
The two-way mirror of life
As we stand dazzled by the light
Of our own reflections,
Blossoming in our self-made greenhouse,
Vital with the signs of spring.
It is the seeds of this love
That determine the life of this love –
Its seasons of growth, strength and beauty
Captured in the summer blooms
Displayed timelessly in the years
Of its maturity.
For those seeds of love,
Prepared with thought and vision,
Sown with understanding,
Nourished with self-sacrifice,
Protected by honest action,
Will flourish into magnificence –
A spectacle of colour and fragrance
For all the world to share.

Such a love
Displays timeless endurance,
Remaining evergreen and fertile,
While the many annual blossoms
From seeds of shallow love
Have vanished without trace.

THE QUALITY OF LIFE

Blue-green, foam-edged seas,
Towering, rainbow hills,
Peaceful, flower-filled gardens
And russet-painted woods.
All these are ours to see,
To ponder on, awestruck,
The unrivalled beauty.
Nature, ever changing,
Robed in splendour,
Magnificent in her display.

Take time to absorb these wonders.
Live every precious moment to the full.
Drink in the perfume
Of the dewy morning rose,
And wonder at the seagull's soaring flight.
Feel the warm, white sand beneath your feet,
Admire the myriads of green,
Rich carpets laid to soothe
And calm and welcome
Those who embrace the treasures of this world.
Time is so precious,
Waste no magic moment
On man's misfortune,
Or dwell in sorrow for what might have been.
Live with the lightness and beauty
Of the butterfly.
Let your heart soar with happiness.
Sing of the joy of being alive
In a world that offers so much beauty
And demands nothing –
Except that you love wholly
All living things
And He who created them.
Love is more precious than life,

It has no boundaries.
It sings from the trees and the shore.
It fills the soul with elation
And emotion is personified.
We are raised up
And filled with radiance
As love is poured in from all that we see
Displayed for our pleasure.
Like a mirror we can reflect
That fathomless love to those around us –
Seeing the beauty of the mind,
Feeling the warmth of affection;
Enjoying the intimacy of sharing
Thoughts, words and tenderness.

Being close in caring silence,
Filling each other with emotion;
Cherishing the magic moments,
Caresses and the sweet embrace;
Walking hand in hand,
Sharing the mystery that the world unfolds –
Treasure all these moments,
Live them to the full.
A life cannot be valued by the span of years
That chains it to a self-made desert.
For the freedom to love unselfishly
And share the natural beauty
Of this chameleon world
Gives life a quality
That no time-span can encompass.

True love makes an ideal existence a reality, it changes daily tasks into treasures and makes service and sacrifice a great joy.

THE SEARCH

For years I searched for the ultimate beauty in the world.
At last I found it –
We carry it in our hearts, our nature,
But rarely is it seen.
I searched for the ultimate truth –
And found it in man's heart
When he is really honest with himself.
I searched for the ultimate love in our world –
I found it in woman's spirit
When she gladly suffers and sacrifices
In an attempt to make the perfect world
For those she loves.
I searched for the ultimate happiness,
A reason for my existence,
And I found it –
My ultimate happiness is knowing you,
Being close to you;
Sharing my thoughts and routine with you.
But my ultimate dream is loving you,
Serving you and making you happy forever.

DISAPPOINTMENT

Some people cause much suffering –
Some people seem to bear all the burdens –
Nothing in this world is ever fairly distributed, or so it seems.

When the downhill path is rough and never ending, be strong and believe that the storms will subside. The results may be a long time coming, but all your efforts will have true value in their own way if you remain true to yourself and your beliefs irrespective of things happening outside your control.

Life is a marathon
Wherein our hopes hide
But love is the leader
With God by our side.

Be at one with nature, absorb her song of love and seek to bring harmony into the lives of others, by understanding that the path of despair leads to hope and the path of sorrow is the path to joy.

TRUST

Let me help you across the river of uncertainty
To the shores of love.
Although the stepping stones
May seem unsteady, almost perilous,
I'll hold you up and not let you flounder,
Guiding you all the way
With love and tenderness,
So that we may go forward together
And face what life has in store.

CRY WOLF

Fire creeps hungrily
Through body, bone and vein
To set my heart ablaze,
Bringing sensations
That confuse and overwhelm me.
I have lived through my days of finest flower,
Seeking perfection in youthful love,
Yet remaining unbending, unknown,
Unfulfilled and unsure of reality.
I aspired to become a Temple of Light,
But within lurked Envy and her sister Jealousy,
Possessiveness, Loss and lingering Pain.
Repeatedly I became a dog
Left licking his wounds.
Reason was never the mistress of Love,
For Love lives on pleasure and distress
And makes me unrecognisable to myself.
Love is elusive, fleeing when touched,
Hiding in the shadows
Of overburdened lives,
Lost in routine.

Passing time has not destroyed my quest.
I am swept along by the new fire of emotions
Surging through my fibres.
I reach out cautiously,
With inhibited joy
To grasp Love's veil –
Afraid it will crumble at my touch.
For despite the reassuring
Interludes of affectionate display,
Warm words of comfort and signs of care –
I walk lightly with outstretched fingers,
Feeling my way,
Hypnotised by the colours
Of my crystal world,
Afraid that it will shatter
Into a thousand pieces, with my dreams,
Leaving my love out in the cold.
How hard it is to believe
That someone really loves me!

ANXIETY

In the middle of a sea of chaos,
Whipped into a storm by the troubles
And problems of our society,
I shall find my island of peace.
With God's love I can withstand
All the buffeting, the philosophies,
The words and actions of those around me.
Together we are an impenetrable rock
That cannot be eroded.
Despite this world and its tortures
Our love will grow strong –
You and I will build our paradise together.

The value of love and loving is often distorted and lost from so many lives. Help is needed to resurrect that love.

THINKING OF YOU

Chuckling water hurrying through the stones,
Singing out memories to my sensitive heart;
Offering foamy bubbles to my searching fingers
Reaching out to touch your hair.
The dancing waters tumbling down the beck
Echo with laughter, and I hear your voice.
I close my eyes in the warmth of the sun,
And dream of log fires, and evenings spent with you.
I curl my toes over the sun-baked turf
And lie back amongst the fragrant bracken
In this natural paradise.
And all is silent except for a solitary bird
Calling mournfully through the evening air,
Sympathising with my incompleteness.
And my whole being
Trembles with longing for your company.
And the riversong becomes a hymn of mourning
For the lost hours and nights,
Now passing by,
Never to be recaptured.
Times of comfort and togetherness
Stolen from us forever –
And my tears fall softly into the water.

FREEDOM

My desires for freedom
Are the shackles that bind me to myself,
For I lock myself away
In the dark prison of my needs.
Striving to remove the burdens of my life,
I bind myself tighter
And feel the torture
Of despair and hopelessness.
Writhing in frustration,
As I centre on myself
And my desire to be free.
For as I remove each burden,
I am confronted with decisions
That chain me tighter to myself.
Freedom is an illusion,
I am my own jailer
In this dark, stale prison.

When I put aside myself –
My needs, my sorrows and desires,
And welcome service to my fellow man,
Without awareness of my physical self;
When I see with Your unselfish eyes,
And feel with Your all-embracing heart;
When I touch my brother with Your love –
Then my spirit soars
Into Your Light –
And I am truly free.

IN SYMPATHY WITH A SEA ANEMONE

Hiding in the shadows,
Attached to my stone that I call home,
I peep out at the world
Through my dark and multi-coloured camouflage.
I sway and drift in time to my surroundings,
Looking and listening and bending under the pressures
Of those around me.
And when the sunlight caresses me in the mornings,
I am lulled into a false sense
Of peace and calm and contentment –
And I unfold,
Stretching out my tentacles into the light,
Reaching out for harmony;
Offering love, comfort and reassurance,
Friendship, understanding and help without reward,
Each fragile tentacle extended –
Towards a fellow being.

Harsh contact! rebuff! anger and malice!
My tentacles recoil in pain, injured.
I withdraw into a self-made cave
To nurse my wounds –
And to regenerate the feeling of emotion,
To regain the strength to offer once more
The gifts of love to mankind –
On cautious tentacles,
To be rejected again.

The power of regeneration is ebbing –
One day I will fall off my rock!

LEARNING

For years I nurtured the seed
And felt the joy–pain of growth within,
And dreamed of happy days to come –
Contentment in the expansion of us.
As the years progressed
The feelings of togetherness grew
In tenderness and understanding
And my femininity blossomed naturally,
Encouraged by attentive care and sweet words.
Physical closeness and completeness
Charged my body with elation,
Fired it with tenderness and unspoken magic
As we melted into a oneness of silent love.
When my spirit was bewildered and hurt
By the world's harsh ways
Your tenderness healed all wounds.
You filled me with hope when I thought all hope was gone.
Sorrow and despair now flood my veins
And I am trying to find a foothold on my crumbling path.
I shall not let you down,
I need a little time to readjust,
Then your love will make me strong again.

MOURNING

There are many beautiful flowers in the garden that will blossom before they fade and die. We must catch them in their beauty and appreciate them wholly while we can, knowing that time is of the essence.

For you can retain the memory of a rose and it will not fade.

According to the nature of things, the flowers in a garden grow and bloom. Some are short lived, others fill the whole season with fragrance.

In winter we must be careful not to mourn the summer rose or we may not see the humble snowdrop lifting its head in all weathers and difficulties to smile at us.

Life is both joyous and sad and the line between is very fine, for we become the harps on which are played the tunes of life and death.

The more you love, the more of the beauty of love and loving is revealed.

IN NATURE'S ARMS I REST

Feel my presence in the warmth of the sunshine
And the vibrant morning air in spring.
Let there be no man-made sign that I have been –
Just memories of my love for all the things alive
Still active in your heart.
When this body has outlived its usefulness
And sets my spirit free,
Then sacrifice it with fire
And scatter my ashes to the wind,
That Nature may embrace me.
When my final hour is come
And my spirit escapes from the shackles that bind it
To its decaying temple,
Let Nature open up her arms
And receive me joyfully.
Let there be no grief or sense of loss,
For a free spirit is in the air,
Absorbed into fragrance
And ever near to comfort earthbound friends.
Let there be no memorial
To attract misplaced sorrow;
No granite statement,
Cold, hard and fleshless,
Unyielding and tormenting –
For that is not me!
See me in the wild flowers,
The thrush's song,
The nodding daffodils,
The smiling dolphin,
The weeping willow.
For I am all these things . . .

REMEMBER ME

Remember me
When salt winds bite the knuckles of the quay.
Remember me
When men have reaped the harvest of the sea.
Remember me
In laughter and the joyous things you see.
Remember me
In thought, in word, at peace, now I am free.
Remember me
With smiles, my love, as I watch over thee . . .

Lowestoft 1986

IN MEMORY OF A FRIEND

I never completely knew this man, my friend.
I heard some of his story,
But the beginning and ending
Were lost to me.
In the fathoms of his heart
Were secrets never to be told,
But what I did know
Made this man my friend.

Understanding grew between myself
And this man, my friend;
Companionship that endured
The ups and downs of life.
Words of comfort, words of advice,
Or a laugh, a joke, a knowing smile
Often I exchanged
With this man, my friend.

The seasons come and go
But a friendship endures all changes,
And my words seem cold and empty now,
Inadequate to express how I feel
When I think of this man, my friend –

So I must trust in silence,
Knowing that he would understand,
And I cherish the memories
That will always linger,
Like footprints in the snow,
Memories of this man, my friend.

DEATH OF A CAT

How can you understand
The hollows freshly dug,
With echoing silence,
Deep into my heart –
And filled with pain and sighs and memories
Of velvet paws and loving looks,
Warmth and comfort and trust.
Echoes of eager welcomes and resounding purrs
Changed from reality to dreams
In an instant of decision –
To let her depart with peace
And dignity,
Her pain exchanged for my grief.
My emotions pay the price for that frail frame
To encompass rest and freedom.
And tears wash away the anguish of despair
And unrealised hopes
As togetherness is aborted
At my reluctant command –
Her suffering is extinguished!

LOVE LOST

Lost and unhappy
You stare at the bones of your life,
Stark, bleached and desolate.
When all you love has faded away
And you cannot face despair,
Then glean among the bones
For one scrap of flesh
To appease your hunger,
Bringing rebirth into sanity.
For on the stormiest overcast day,
One ray of sunshine shafting through
Has more brilliance
Than the hottest summer day.
Among suffocating weeds,
One tiny flower will struggle and grow
And live out its cycle in beauty.
Despair is the path to hope;
Accepting where you are
Sets you on the new path
Out of the maze of unhappiness.
Open your eyes to the beauties of Creation.
Dwell on things beyond man
And his destructive nature.
Pause with the plants
And share their slow understanding
Of being alive.
Then, in a while,
With renewed energy and hope
You will continue your struggle.
Your emotions will heal
And you face a new life –
With a deeper knowledge of yourself.

ANOTHER TIME, ANOTHER PLACE

Another time, another place
Where I may look
Upon thy face.
For this the astral robe is mine –
If I would pass the fence of time
And so set my spirit free.
Freedom to respond, express,
And wander unrestricted
From the inhibited corpse
Of this lifetime.
Loose the shackles of society –
And be!

I am light particles
In the ray of the source
Of the Great Spirit,
Drifting upwards on the tide of emotion.
Supreme elation!
Our emotions will entwine
Bodiless!
Our Eden –
Must be in the realms of space.
And our fate –
To be prisoners
In this place!

REMEMBRANCE

Delicate poppy –
Satin smooth,
Feminine softness
Of curved crimson petals.
Unrivalled beauty sparkling
Like a ruby in the golden harvest,
Or leaping out from lush, green banks
Along our winding roads,
Clamouring for attention!

In your face
Is expressed the memory
Of long-ago sorrow.
The blood of the battlefield,
And the nameless dead
Scattered, like your seeds,
Into Mother Earth
To nurture the hopes of tomorrow.

Frail little flower,
Standing alone,
Bending and crushed
By the elements, the harvester
And ignorant feet;
Yet rising up anew
In fertile earth each Spring,
Scattering your life blood
Throughout this land.
A constant reminder
That when man engages in war
Then sacrifice
Is the price we pay for peace.

THE SHELL LIVES ON

I am an empty shell,
Devoid of feeling and emotion,
Numb to the noises of life around me,
Tossed about on the shore by the tides of life;
Holding captive the echoing whispers
Of the past,
The sighs of love and happiness lost,
Memories re-echoing in my spiral shell,
Awaiting a curious listener.

The heart that beat,
The mind that thought,
The emotions that felt,
The pulse that raced,
All suspended –
Cremated
And scattered to the wind
That roars within,
Trapped in the spiral shell.

But the shell lives on,
Drifting with the ocean
Known as humanity.

THOUGHTS FROM HOLLIE

Aged 6 years, Norwich 1986

No hours or years can entrap me,
My spirit is free as a bird.
I shine in the sparkle of raindrops
And drink from the dew on the grass.
I glow in the light of the rainbow
And skip with the lambs in the Spring.
I'm the bright-eyed daisy of Summer
And the touch of a butterfly's wing.
In God's classroom we learn many lessons –
How to cherish each moment we're there,
We learn the true meaning of family
And we learn what it means to care.
I learned a whole lifetime of loving,
Felt the joy of the brightest of dreams.
My heart sang with a deep understanding,
God's love touched me through every sunbeam.
God sent us the fairies of knowledge
And we learned how to give with our hearts,
The time that we had was so precious,
Our love will see we are never apart.

At Christmas time when you trim the tree
And it shines like magic –
Remember me!
In my name pick bright, green holly
With berries so rich and warm;
I shall smile from every glossy leaf
And share your peace and calm.

Let your memories create a garden of joy
With the brightest flowers you've ever seen.
Let happy thoughts guide you, put sorrow away
For the spirit of Hollie remains evergreen.

THE WINGS OF FREEDOM

I soar on the wings of freedom,
Hovering under the warm sun,
Drinking in the green fields
And the warm browns of the wood below.
The breeze carries me gently,
And I dart and dive
In a wilderness of Paradise,
Plucking the blood-red berries;
Pausing, listening, watching
The busy life all around me.
And I burst into song,
As my nimble mind is captured
By thoughts of nests
And eggs and summer.
And joyously I soar
Towards the arms of a nearby tree,
Oblivious of the green monster
Bearing down,
Eating up the road below me.
Little heart pounding –
Alert too late!
A hollow thud –
Gone are the wings of freedom,
And the memory of my song
Echoes down the wind.

MEMORIES

When I think of you I feel a warm glow of happiness.
I think of the nights, snuggling close,
Warm and contented.
I think of the evenings, exchanging thoughts and problems
And sharing our views of the world.
I think of our walks, discovering the natural beauty
God has created,
Time spent consoling each other
On the evidence of man's destructiveness.
I want to touch your face,
Look into your eyes
And tell you again that I love you.
You gave me so much to live for –
Feelings that I never thought were possible.
You shared your emotion and your secrets,
Your heartaches and your dreams.
I am glad for I have become a part of you.
You are my life's blood.
I shall live on, steeped in memories,
Following the path we started to explore.
One day we will rediscover our happiness
Together.

DETERMINATION

It is not how much time we have here that matters, it is what we do with our time. Life must have meaning.

Problems and burdens arise to sharpen our spirit. Illness and injustice are situations in which we become the unexpected victim or sacrifice. The secret is not to run away but to advance towards it, take it in your stride, do not falter. Rise triumphantly above it, not allowing the situation to alter your resolute nature in any way. Continue on with renewed strength – that is victory. Pause in a silent garden or the countryside and inhale the life force so evident in the beauty of the natural environment. Feel the strength within. Draw on divine strength to give *you* the strength to face your problems and let love convince you that you can move mountains. Positive thoughts get positive results. A frail body can indeed house a strong spirit. Mind over matter can be an all too familiar battle – but it works!

BEGINNINGS

Only when your heart is broken
Can you really begin to love.
Only when you have suffered pain and sorrow
Can you really understand joy.
Only when you are unhappy
Can you begin to feel true happiness.
This is the time to build a new life
With resolution.

THE BREATH OF LOVE

I watched from the shadow of myself
As dusk crept like a cautious cat,
Silently, across the rippling green of the garden,
And my thoughts centred on you.
In my imagination you shone like the brightest star –
And I, like a moth around a flame,
Fluttered crazily, beating my wings,
Repelled by the heat, but returning, unheeding,
Drawn unresisting towards the light –
Mesmerised –
Preferring to be engulfed by the flame
Than exist, unfulfilled,
In the selfish shadows of myself.

So this is love!
The agonising joy of self-willed sacrifice
That desires true happiness for another soul.
As I battle through the stormy, grief-heavy clouds,
Shafts of rainbow-coloured ecstasy
Pierce my heart –
And we are one,
In an all-embracing moment of infinite brightness.

Without love
Life is like the raw, imperfect clay
That sleeps in the ground
Before the sculptor prepares it,
Moulds it and breathes
The breath of the Creator into it.

I am an artist and sculptor,
And I cherish and care for the clay.
Prepare it with love and understanding,
Nourish it –
Breathing life from my very soul
Into its heart.
So that it may metamorphosise,
Like a phoenix arising from the ashes,
To love reborn.

MY LOVE FOR YOU

My love for you
Begins with a spark of light in my soul,
Shining like a solitary candle in a darkened room.
On delicate wings that light spirals forth,
Filling my being, radiating brightest sunshine
Which envelops you.
Hold me close –
Let me sense your love
Penetrating my frail bones.
Let us seal our special bond of love
And build it stronger,
That we may face the problems of the future
And dissolve them in love.

LIGHT IN THE DARKNESS

I am the tiniest drop of water,
Insignificant in the teeming water of the beck –
The flowing water of humanity
That rushes noisily among the boulders of life,
Eroding tradition,
And scattering small stones –
New ideas unheard, untested –
As it clumsily stumbles onwards
With determined, self-concerning mind;
One established mass of confidence
Preying on Nature standing watchful on the banks,
And drawing in fresh streamlets
To expand its strength.

Yet those free spirits,
Watching with hopeful eyes,
Will see the waters rise and fall,
Finding their own ways among the ageless rocks;
Separating into foaming splendour,
Leaping up from the waters,
Creating little pools,
Calm and still,
Reflecting the fresh greens and fragrance
Of a vibrant life
Touched by the Creator.
And in the early morning glow
Tiny droplets emerge
On velvet mossy banks
And sparkle – jewels of individuality;
Diamonds of light and hope for all mankind,
And pearls of sorrow and understanding.
Each droplet willingly evaporates
Into the Oneness,
Its natural form discarded,
Long separated from the flow of selfishness.

Each individual force
Fuses with the light,
Adding to its warmth and brightness.
And with one loving, caring mind
Shines down upon the dwindling river
That more may be uplifted,
And only the stony bones be left dry –
As a warning and reminder
Of what man once was.

AWAKENING

All my life
My heart has been a tight, spring bud,
Veiling the hopes, dreams and promises
Of fragrant blossom.
Since I have known God
My heart has opened
Petal by petal,
Shaking off fear and sorrow,
Growing daily stronger
In the sunshine of His love.

Let the love in your heart keep growing and endeavour to make your actions the fruit of the seeds in your heart.

TIME TO THINK

Illness is never welcome yet, in terms of a whole life's activity, being out of circulation for a while can be a blessing. It gives one an opportunity to unwind all the agitation and unrest in the inner self and get rid of it forever. When the pressure and stress of an active working life is removed, there is time to listen to your thoughts and experience fully the feelings in your heart.

It can be good just once in a while to stop and listen to the grass grow.

Spending hours in listening silence is like waking from a deep sleep and breathing fresh air. There is time to think things out and come to terms with yourself, your ways, and your ideas. Time to question 'why' about so many aspects that you suddenly have to face about yourself. Until we come to terms with ourselves we cannot hope to understand others and see from their point of view.

If we receive criticism, rather than reject it in a reflex way, or get angry, it is more beneficial to consider the criticism and cross-examine ourselves and our behaviour. It is often possible to make a positive attempt to modify and change our behaviour once we have admitted a truth about our failings.

Thoughts are the seeds of words, nourish them only when you are sure that they will produce beautiful blossoms.

MORNING GREETING

Good morning, lake!
Stretching out in crisp coolness
In a comforting curve around me,
Your soft beauty veiled in modesty
By the trees that fringe your shore,
Watched over by your guardian
That towers behind you,
With dark and disciplined peaks,
In fatherly tones,
Hugging you to his slopes.
Beautiful lake,
Like a shy bride, welcoming morning,
Nestling into the comforting arms
Of green-robed Pan.
Relaxed and shimmering
Beneath the bright counterpane
Of the cloud-scattered sky.
Still waters in silent contentment,
Embracing peace.

A SECRET PLACE

The lapping of the waves
Was the lullaby
That hummed softly
Beyond the warm wind's whistle.
She danced over the hills,
Tugging at the twisting forest
Of heather roots,
Sweeping over the bald patches
Shining stone pink on the summit.
The heather clusters crowd together
In their gregarious way,
Enveloping the sea hills.
The flower spires
Shake vigorously in the breeze
That sweeps down into secret hollows
Glowing purple in a dense mattress
Of inviting comfort.
The secluded bower,
Enriched by moments of affection,
Murmurs softly –
Incantations
Of the magic of dreams.

AN AFTERNOON IN THE DALES

The sky was a calm, waveless sea
As we gazed upwards into the still sunshine.
Resting on a grassy mound
We fell asleep,
Serenaded by the shy and curious sheep nearby.
We felt the mist on our faces
As we scrambled up stony tracks,
Leaping over rain-sodden turf.

Nature's wonderland unfolded
In a full-length epic of colour and fragrance.
'These are stinging nettles,' you announced.
To compete with my own observations.
We breathed the serenity of the countryside
As we walked in understanding silence,
Or chatted and laughed at ourselves,
Keeping company with Mother Nature in all her moods.

HYMN TO WALES

The white waters sing hymns of praise
As they leap from rock to rock
In swirling torrents
Tumbling joyfully down to the heart of the valley.
The proud, purple mountains reach for the clouds
Through their flowing cloaks of flower-studded greens
That ripple into folds between still, blue lakes
Which sparkle like jewels as they reflect
The face of their Creator.

Beneath the nodding daffodils
On the sheep-grazed hills
A hard, black heart beats loudly,
Beckoning her people, enticing them
Into her ebony arteries,
To toil like ants unerground.
Here the Welsh character is etched
Into coal-black faces
As it has been for generations.
The earth shakes with the sound of Celtic voices
Echoing across the centuries,
Praising God for His gifts, His love,
And the air that they breathe –
Proud protectors of their native land.

THE MARBLE QUARRY, IONA

The frame stands rigid,
Staring over the forgotten marble blocks
Heaped untidily on the shore.
The stark lines of the frame
Enfold the sea view,
Its cutting teeth long blunted and decayed.
It is a silent mouth,
Nibbling at the marble long forgotten.
The engine lies broken, hard against the cliff,
Its hunger for coke now a forgotten famine
And its gases long lost in the bracing air.
The drive shaft lies idly in its bearings,
Its length now pitted
By the hot, angry breath of rust.
The clanking of activity is an echo across the decades.
The cliff sides soar up,
Ravaged by cuboid bites of long ago,
Welcoming the hands of the sea
Reaching for the rusty metal shapes
In a determined effort
To destroy all traces of man.

CHANGES

The hymns of praise are silent,
The whispered prayers are hushed,
The congregation's murmurings
Are echoes of the past.
These stones that make the House of God
Vibrate with ageless love,
Sheltering the worshippers
And comforting the sad.
For man has walked within these walls
For many a year and more,
Giving voice to understanding,
Sharing love as he entered the door.

Though God's face is eternally changeless
And His love the foundation stone,
Man changes his ways with the seasons –
The centuries mould him anew.
His spirit bursts out of convention,
Beliefs are a lively display.
His soul feels the depth of Creation
As back to God's gifts he returns.

This church has not been forgotten.
Not here will there be hollow sighs!
But a sharing of skills and love's labours –
For this is the stage, for man's joys.
The heart of this church is still beating,
Many people will come with their crafts.
Come home to a joyous appraisal
Of the bond between Father and Man!

St Gregory's Church, Norwich

TIME ON THE BEACH

Warm sand trickling between my toes
Like a hungry hourglass gnawing
At the precious moments of our afternoon together.
That stolen interlude upon the contented shore,
Walking hand in hand, oblivious to man.
Suspended in time –
Talking,
Of taxes and costs and consciences,
Man's greed, deceit and selfishness,
Expressing our views and sharing ideas.
Only an Alsatian broke into our thoughts,
Bouncing playfully along,
Beautiful and carefree, contrasting with man.

And the gentle waves danced before a clear horizon,
The warm breeze caressed us
As you picked up a stone and gave it to me –
A fossilised sea urchin, once a simple, natural creature,
That had left its mark upon the world
So that we might know that it had lived here once.
We shared a timeless moment in millions of years.

I thought about our discussion of modern man.
Would our society leave such a lasting impression
As the timeless sea urchin?
Hopefully, like our footsteps in the sand –
It will vanish without trace!

ENGLAND

For St George's Day 1985

The dew is singing in the grass
And the trumpets of daffodils
Sound a golden fanfare.
The birds in the hedgerow
Sing loudly above.
The rhythm of raindrops
Fading after a storm.
This is the symphony of creation
Resounding throughout the cathedral
That is England.
Tall trees, finely sculptured,
Standing in dignified avenues,
Make timeless arches,
Weaving a canopy
Over the altars of our heritage –
The fragrant gardens we tend with care,
The bluebell-carpeted woods,
The fields of buttercups,
The crimson-poppied banks,
And diamond-studded streams.
This is our house of prayer –
The place prepared for this nation
To walk and talk and commune
With the Breath of Love
Who created all things.
Man creates temples with brick and stone
In an attempt to confine His presence,
But He has created this land
As His temple,
In which to welcome us.
An emerald, sparkling land,
Ever alive and adorned anew each year
In beautiful robes of mountain heather,

Autumn leaves,
Daisyed meadows and frosty hedgerows.
A place in which to worship
And love all things.

TARN HOWS

I melt into the earth
And absorb the fragrance of the bracken.
I sparkle in the light
Of the ripples on the tarn.
I stand weathered on the hill –
Immovable rock,
Gazing out to rocky crags –
And I stand tall with the spruce
Reaching for the sky.
Mystically I am drawn to this place.
It is the first and last place in my heart.
I linger by the still waters
That reflect the face
Of my Creator.
Here at Tarn Hows
I am one with God.
He overwhelms, yet comforts me.
I embrace the silent earth
And my 'self' fades away.

Lake Coniston

CONTINUATION . . .

It is time to take the first, faltering steps
Up the path of retirement,
Approaching in trepidation
The unfolding secrets of new experiences
And a different routine.
The first day of your new era
Will find you poised with anticipation
With the identical feelings that absorbed you
The day you started your first job
When you embarked on an unknown world.
Pause now upon your path
And listen to the song echoing from the past.
A melody was created by you
Through words, thoughts and deeds
As you travelled along life's highway.
You have made many friends
In whose hearts has been carved a place for you
And the memory of you.
You now have time to pause, dream and savour memories;
Time to look around you at the wonders
That the hurrying eye does not see.
You have time to care for all those
Who are fortunate to stray onto your path.
This is a time to learn, a time to share,
A time to ponder, a time to create new memories.
Most of all it is a time for wisdom.
For honest reflection on our lives
Helps us to discover who we are
And our place in the order of things.
This knowledge makes us masters of our destiny
And brings peace, contentment and joy
That nourishes our soul –
As we embark on the adventure of retirement.

BENEDICTION

I kneel in the green cathedral of my garden,
My heart expanded by Your presence.
My peace is challenged
By Your feathered choir
Singing Your praises
With their songs of humility.
Nature echoes with a holy harmony.
The earth vibrates with quickening growth.
I am one with the dust,
I melt into the grass –
Leaving an empty vessel
To be filled with Your love.

I believe that all things are possible if you have faith, patience and sincerity.

POSITIVE THOUGHT AND ILLNESS

Negative attitudes often seem unavoidable, but unless we change them we make no progress.

Strength of mind is needed to deal with life's problems. When we encounter bad situations it is our job to change them into good situations. It is how we deal with a situation that really matters. For example, if we find that we are suffering from a serious illness, how do we cope with the situation? We learn to see life from a very different point of view and all our experiences within that illness will teach us something more and add to our understanding. One needs to attempt an honest analysis of the situation in realistic terms, also an analysis of one's feelings on the matter. Facing the basic facts of existence will formulate new meanings in one's life. The soul is very pliable.

If you are very ill your world shrinks rapidly. You are no longer concerned with work, shopping, decorating your home, or gardening. Interests and people vanish from your world and very often the end of the bed is the boundary of existence. Lack of sleep, pain and discomfort, cause a hazy, dreamlike existence. Within your shrunken world everything becomes magnified and important. An object near to you, a flower, a shape, seems to absorb your whole being. Physical existence can become overbearingly dominant. Actions which usually pass unnoticed, such as breathing in and out, moving, eating, sleeping, become suffocating functions; they absorb your mind. If the body is very weak you cannot physically do much to alter your state, but you can use your mind. Then recognise your helplessness, look for inner strength and start to fight back. This is the time to draw on spiritual strength.

If you take each aspect of your existence and try to deal with it in a positive way your whole life changes. You need determination and inner strength in dealing with your attitude to life, whether it is illness or another problem.

Our attitude to pain, when we are ill, is very important for it is our body dictating almost to the extent of what we think, let alone what we do, and it completely restricts our lives.

It is not easy to be positive with pain, but it is possible. In stages you can deal with pain by using your mind to keep it in its place and not allow it all the victory. Mind over matter is a true saying. You can dictate to your body the desires of your mind, with the clear goal that once you can push yourself to one side you can begin to think about other people, their problems, and so take your place in the order of things once more.

Remember that optimism keeps you one step ahead of every problem.

All the poems in this section were written in the hazy world of serious illness.

ISLAND PEACE

I am drawn into a vacuum
Of an incredible silence,
A deep chasm of peace
That absorbs the landscape
And all living things.
Sheep graze,
Rabbits leap and tumble,
Grass and flowers grow
Unheard.
And the silence echoes on
As the amazed onlooker
Listens for the sounds of life,
Which are mysteriously suppressed.

ISLE OF HARRIS

I am absorbed into the stillness
Of the scented air.
I am woven into the textured heathers
In mingling clumps
On uneven rocks.
I am blended into the delicate hues
Of flower-saturated heath.
I am inhaled by the island's beauty –
And the lonely seagull's cry
Is the song in my soul.

AWARENESS

Over the rabbit-ridden dunes
Where endless warrens gape,
Nervous sheep graze,
Often startled by an invisible terror
That stirs them to leap
And dash in all directions
As seabirds utter their melancholy cries
In protest.
The echoing notes float upwards
Into the moaning wind
That carries the sound through the oncoming mist
That appears from nowhere,
Shrouding the land,
Blotting out the islands
And weeping on the silent turf.

PAIN

Pain is my keeper
Who disciplines my life.
From time to time he lulls me
Into a sense of false elation –
Relaxing his hold a little,
Giving me the illusion that I am free
And my own master.
Then reining in,
He displays his strength and power
And I am his captive again,
Forced to dance to his tune,
Twisting and turning,
Trying to escape his unbending grip.

Sometimes I challenge him,
Remaining motionless
In forced relaxation;
Using my mind to transform his onslaught
Into waves that flow from me
To be absorbed into the air.
But the echoes seem to bombard me
Like the backlash of turbulent waters –
Exposing my fragility,
Re-imposing his will.
I am brought to heel, bowing to his strength,
Unable to outrun him.
I acknowledge his superior strength
Inwardly.
But his victory is a song unsung,
For I retain my composure
By silence.

THE VIEW BEYOND MY PAIN

The white rollers
Are tossing their heads restlessly
And snorting up the shore,
Their green backs merging
Into the heaving, grey mantle
Stretching to the horizon.
Leaping with the joy of freedom,
The waves rear up noisily
And pound upon the shore,
Gnawing hungrily at
The smooth, yellow sand
Beyond the still, quiet slopes
Of the rabbit-clad dunes.

Illness takes away energy, pain interferes with peace of mind. Life becomes a clutter of physical and emotional distractions, but determination and love lead to victory.

VIEW FROM A HOSPITAL WINDOW

All I can see is a red brick wall,
Angry and inflamed,
Harsh upon my eyes.
My gaze wanders
In a hypnotic way,
Following the channelled lines of mortar;
A crumbling maze of angles
That draws me to follow
Along and upwards in a mechanical way.
I seem unable to stop this exercise.
My eyes are constantly drawn
To the pale, straight lines,
And I stumble along looking for a way to escape,
Away from the rusty blocks
And their cemented tracks.
I long for a glimmer of blue sky
And the curves of ever-changing clouds.
I am imprisoned by the moods of these bricks
That change with the weather;
Forbidding and dark on a cloudy day
Or soaking up the rain like the flanks of an enormous beast
Whose outline is out of view.
On sunny days the bricks are bright,
Demanding attention all day long,
Drawing my gaze into the weathered channels.
The monotony depresses me,
My eyes are tired mirrors.
I long for the darkness
When the night swallows up
The view from my window.

JEAN McCLEOD

She sits, propped on pillows,
Swaddled in blankets,
Eyes alert, staring through the open door
For the signs of activity
That indicate the rhythm of life;
Waiting for moments of routine
That will create landmarks of time,
And give orientation to the struggling heartbeat.
Her face like wrinkled parchment,
Gnarled by decades of hardship
And weathered by the salty island air –
Grimaces, changing shape with explosive coughing,
Shaking the frail frame into spasms of activity.
The noise, magnetic, attracts a caring head,
Popped enquiring round the door.
Soft Gaelic flows musically between the two,
The wizened crofter
And the young nurse.
Then silence again.
The breathless, grey-haired form
Crumples wearily into slumber.
Purple-veined, misshapen hands,
Now naked and idle –
Separated from their usual task
Of knitting Harris socks –
Are hooked onto the blankets.
Her mind escapes from time and place
And she recaptures her youth;
Relives the excitement
Of her days as a herring girl,
Clothed in oilskins and wellingtons,
Packing the fish barrels
Among the noise and bustle
On the busy quay at Yarmouth.
And the time-worn frame

Heaves and flounders restlessly,
But slumbers determinedly on!

THE X-RAY

Gently slid to and fro,
Arranged upon the couch
Beneath the winking eye
Of the metal monster
Poised as if to pounce
Upon the vulnerable flesh below.
Breathing is controlled
By command
As the machine whirrs into action,
Shuddering to a click
Of decision.
The explorer,
White coated and resolute,
Dares to seek the darkest depths
Of my being – yet unviewed;
Capturing the negative truth,
Revealing its secret
On the dazzling screen
Which draws him
Like a moth to a flame.
And seeing all,
He utters diagnosis
In the manner of ancient incantations,
Heralding the revelation
Of the steps to a solution –
The path back to health.

THE FORGOTTEN ONES

Dark, grey skin
Like stale, uncooked pastry,
Rolled and draped over fleshless bones,
Brittle and stretched over every contour.
Only a faded flicker of blue
In the sunken skull,
And the occasional eerie wail
Denotes life.
With loving care the shape
Is heaved and altered
Like a flexible toy;
Powdered and groomed
And comforted;
Addressed with dignity –
And the visual nightmare
For a short space of time
Retains serenity.

SIGNS OF SPRING

If pain is to be my shadow
Then I shall outshine him,
Condemn him to walk, veiled,
A dark pace behind me.
I shall keep my face in the sunshine
As I stride along life's path –
So full of promise and beautiful tomorrows.
I shall turn deaf ears and silence
To pain's pleading for recognition.
And though he follows me closely,
Pushing his way into my activities,
I shall contain him –
Banish him to the corner of my mind.
Never will he again dictate my path
Or divert me from my pleasures.
For he is destined to become
My unwilling companion,
Dominated by my will to live life
To the full.
I shall be my own mistress,
Uncompromising in my endeavour
To love and live a new life –
Strengthened by God's love.

I shall create light in every grey day
And ride the rainbow of expanding joy.
Pain will become the reluctant follower,
Robbed of the limelight of acknowledgement.
Humbled by God's strength and love
Flowing into my soul,
Activating my will.

I am in command, Spring has begun!

LOVE IS GREEN

The green growth of our world is prompted by the force of love. This concerns our place in the order of things and the harmony of the environment. A parallel seems to exist between the growth of ourselves, our spiritual progress and the natural cycles one finds among plants in their natural habitat.

A gardener at work tries to achieve control, balance and beauty. He plays the role of creator, selecting seeds and plants and planting them to achieve the patterns and designs that he has decided on. He removes weeds and prunes back vigorous growth to achieve quality. He tries to provide a beautiful environment to share with others.

Here there is a comparison with his own spiritual growth for he is also the creator of his developing soul. Given the right ingredients his body will grow naturally, but it is how he thinks and what he does that moulds his soul. He has many choices but he can create his soul in a similar way to his garden. He has to take responsibility for himself and his spiritual progress.

We are all very small and insignificant and yet we are a part of a very large, eternal blueprint in which plants, animals and people all play their vital part. Each has an important part to play and each is dependent on the others for harmony and balance in the environment.

LOVE IS GREEN

The feathery fingers of the silver birch
Beckon me
Into the green of the garden.
The juniper, proud and dark,
Stands in silent wisdom
Among the multi-greens
That offer up bright-eyed blossom
For her approval.
Tulips stand to attention
By clumps of daffodils
Nodding informally
To the fragrant rosemary.
The lawn stretches out a welcome,
Enticing me with a vibrant mantle
Encrusted with diamond-sparkling dew.
I am drawn into the peace
And lulled by the fragrance
All around me;
Caressed by delicate blossoms
Quivering in the breeze,
Entranced by crimson paeonies
And serenaded by a choir of velvet bees.
The plants sing out with happiness,
Opening their arms to each other,
Snuggling together,
Creating a vibrant carpet
Woven with new life
Nourished by the brown earth.
Serenity and harmony prevail
And my soul absorbs the wonder
In the silence of Spring's love song.
My heart sings with joy,
Sharing the secret
That love is green.

GARDEN COLOURS

My soul is like my garden
Blossoming forth
With the Spring,
Full of hopes of maturing
With the passing seasons;
Filled with new life
Stretching forth in bud
To enhance the design
Of the garden.
My heart reaches out
To captivate the senses,
Offering understanding and comfort,
Blending with the environment,
In simple peace.
Some gardens will never feel
The gaze of appreciating eyes,
They bloom in forgotten splendour.

Give constantly to love and you shall receive ultimate joy.

PARADISE

My words and actions
Are the fruit and blossom of my thoughts,
My thoughts the seeds
That determine the blossom.
From within I create the garden
In which I am destined to live
And to prepare for those I love.
From the mind can spring the nurtured seeds
Of colour, form and fragrance,
Untold beauty and variety,
That capture the senses
And bathe them in peace, joy and serenity,
Creating the Garden of Eden.
From an honest heart clear fountains spring
That rain on fish of purest gold,
Silent, graceful and arresting
In their gentle beauty.
From unselfish thoughts
The perfect rose blooms,
Diamond studded in the morning dew.
From self-denial the fragrance of freesias
And orange blossom constantly fills the air.
From care and understanding grow
Carpets of delicate shades and colours.
From contentment grow the many greens of peace
In the shade of cool foliage.
This is the exquisite paradise in which I long to dwell
And share with those I love,
Bathed in the sunshine of happiness.
Let not the seeds of material longings,
Selfish needs, desires or demands
Enter my heart.
For then the mildew of envy

And the blight of jealousy
Would attack my thoughts.
I dread to live in a nightmare garden,
Choked with the strangling tendrils and roots
Of the ever-hungry weeds of despair
That would suffocate my soul
And shut out the light from my garden,
Transforming it into a dark, lonely jungle
That all will abandon.
Let me always be aware
That I am the creator
Of Heaven or Hell on earth,
And that giving must blossom before taking.
For I am the harvester
Of the fruits
From the seeds that I sow.

THE BRIDLE PATH IN WINTER

Mine is the peace
Of the bright, green field carrying me away,
The sculptured furrows
Of multi-brown crags that follow
The line of the twisting road,
The fields like giant patchwork
Sewn untidily together
By uneven hedges.
The twisted arms of the hedgerow,
Clad in their ivy cloaks,
Shake their dead fingers at us
As we ride by.
Hoof beats rhythmically pound the road
And dissolve into waves of oak leaves
Swishing and lapping around us.
Bright puddles reflect dazzling clouds
Catching my pony's eye,
Making him dart sideways
Into the squelchy mud and yesterday's leaves.
All is still
As we hurry along an avenue
Lined with firs
That have avoided many Christmasses.
Now standing at attention
They watch us go by.
A pheasant breaks the silence,
Whirring upwards, uttering cries,
And we both jump with surprise.
The afternoon draws in,
Painting the sky with vivid pinks.
We quicken our pace,
Eating up the road as it uncoils before us,
Then canter across the stubble of yesterday's harvest,
Heading for home.

YORKSHIRE WALLS

Adorned in harebell blue,
The bright walls
Struggle slowly upwards
In grass-strewn strides,
Meandering through a flowery paradise
Of yellow globes and purple vetch
And a myriad of pinks, blues and greens;
Silently wending their way
Between proud thistles
Standing to attention
In every pasture.
Black-faced sheep snuggle
Along the stony flanks,
Basking in the sunshine
Or sheltering from the rain.
With timeless patience
The stones stand firm,
Encumbered with ladders, gates and stiles
Welcoming the rambler,
Pointing out the scenery
And tirelessly keeping pace
With every climber
Up and down and across the Dales;
Straddling the landscape,
Framing the meadows,
Displaying Nature's beauty
In a vast, stone gallery.

RAIN IN THE DALES

The steady trickle of raindrops
Gyrating in pools beneath my window
Mingles harmoniously
With the gentle surge of the Wharfe
As it meanders its way through the dale,
Slithering over the protruding stones,
White and bleak as parched bones,
On the dried up river bed.
And black roads
Like gnarled fingers
Stretch out from Kettlewell,
Carrying wet and weary travellers
Onwards, away from her timeless face.
Only the sheep-sheltering walls
Are climbing the slippery hills
Into the grey, misty mantle of cloud
Shrouding the brow.
And clear water gushes
From new wounds
And angrily rushes
Over rocks and roots,
Snaking downwards to the lower slopes,
Disappearing among the huddling cattle.
And the rain continues its endless song.

BROOKE CHURCHYARD

The round tower pressed against the sky
Stretches up from the sleepy church
And looks across the labelled ground
To the ancient yew.
Dark, green, impenetrable growth
That ignores the elements,
Standing stoutly,
Peeping over the warm brick wall
Into the gardens nearby.
A sveldt, black cat
Glides between the stones,
Alert for movement of life
Among the dead;
Waiting for the unwary mole
To leave its underground tomb;
Or reckless, scampering mouse –
Or hungry bird intent on worms
In a worm's paradise.
Among the granite reminders
Of lives extinguished,
That cluster at sinister angles,
Throwing shadows across uneven turf –
The cat strikes!
The arena echoes
With the victim's death cries,
Shattering the heavy silence
That pervades the churchyard.
Then all is still.
The cat bounds off, prey in mouth.
Darkness smothers echoes of death.
The watching tower tolls the bells,
Blotting out the nightly carnage
Of luminous-eyed creatures,
And the graves devouring the dead.

CORMORANTS

Midnight feathers gleaming
On outstretched wings
Ruffled by the salt breeze.
Elegant neck curved upwards
In an arc,
The cormorant stands, bright eyed,
Watching, a sentry on his rock,
Silhouetted against the blue sky.
The sheer, gnarled rocks,
Black and sinister,
Rise up from angry seas
Swirling round their feet.
A chasm eating its way harshly
Into the gentle green
Of the sheep-flecked hills above.
On every tiny ledge
Of the black fortress
Rested the splayed, webbed feet
Of the waiting cormorants.
A colony of life relaxing
In a rugged, inhospitable
Cathedral of harsh immovable blackness.
Water dripped rhythmically
On a curious and unsuspecting head
Held to one side in constant surprise.
Groups of birds flew in
Low over the waves,
Necks outstretched –
The sea swans of the rocky shore,
Landing effortlessly on the narrow ledges.
Blending into the black rocks
Until only the glint of the sun
On yellow beak and sharp eye
Exposes their dark fortress
To the curious intruder.

FIONNPHORT

Dressed in her pink, granite robe,
She settles in the sun,
Arranging her flounces on the shore,
Cradling the cattle that gaze out to sea
Munching the contentment of evening
Along with the cud.
Only the ferry ruffles her skirt
As it shunts to and fro,
Herding the wide-eyed, blinkered people
'Passing through'
With hardly a glance
At the white sand sparkling
Among the pink curves of her rocky attire.

FINGAL'S CAVE

Staffa, regurgitated from the belly of Time,
A monument erected from Mull's lava flow.
A multitude of pillars arise
From tesselated paving
Encrusted with sea life –
Yet still black from Mull's hot breath.
From the yawning mouth along the causeway
Resound the weird notes of a dirge
Played by the sea.
It echoes through the cave,
Climbing its cathedral walls
Like the strains of a funereal choir.
A crescendo of notes –
Keening from the lost monks –
Engulfs the unwary intruder
With its siren's song.

ISLE OF ERISKA

Island of beautiful silence,
Disturbed by my trespassing feet
Scattering chuckling stones
On the ever-changing shore.
Still waters
With a murmuring fringe
Lick at the crouching rocks
And startled gulls take flight
With piercing cry –
Shattering the silence.
The slopes grow rusty
With the ageing bracken,
And heather roots
Like dead men's fingers
Grasp my moving feet.
A mantle of brown envelops the beach –
Seaweed, holding captive
Tired autumn leaves.
Sculptured rocks
Guard the shores,
Dressed in saffron lichen
Trimmed with palest green;
While black stones
Stare from mirrored waters
Reflecting the sepia mountains
And the glory of the setting sun
Through silhouetted trees.

Argyllshire

GLENSANDA

The birth of a quarry

Glensanda's face
Is blushing pink with pride
As she awakes from centuries
Of sleep
To greet
Man's attentive gaze
And becomes his bride,
Rolling back her green locks,
Exposing the treasures
Of her heart.
Yellow metal creatures
Perch on ledges,
Craning and arching their necks
In constant activity,
Mimicking the preening cormorants
That stand sentry nearby.
On the rosy cliff
Are steps
Hewn by man
For giant feet
To stride the hills.
The granite heart is throbbing
As new arteries
Spring to life
And stone pours forth
For man to utilise.
And when the time
For leaving comes

Then man and land
Will part as friends.
The waves will lap about her feet,
The islands watch her go to sleep.
Green drapes will fall towards the shore,
Covering her secret for evermore.

Argyllshire

JOURNEY FROM STORNOWAY

Wild and rugged beauty,
Untamed and uncontrolled.
An unbending landscape
Shouting out its unchanging nature.
Towering hills, rock faced
And sparse of green,
Penetrated only by leaping streams
Resolutely surging over dark boulders.
Undulating green slopes,
Rippled with the uneven ridges
Of old peat diggings
Now overgrown –
Except for gaping hollows
In which the black-faced sheep
Snuggle to escape the biting winds
That roar down to the numerous
Sparkling lochs,
Tearing up the wet surface
With merciless talons.
Rugged and treeless,
Lewis displays her timeless magnificence.

SCARISTA

Murmuring blue sea
Lace edged upon the shore,
Whispering memories of yesterday –
Of whaling ships,
Stark and foreboding,
Silently sailing out
On their dark missions.
Timeless sea,
Neatly tucked in
Around the meandering shore
Of Toe Head,
Sharing secrets with the gentle slopes
That stand proud,
Protecting the bay from Atlantic gales.
The air is filled
With nostalgic murmurings
Of crofters toiling,
Spinning, weaving,
And black shapes
Putting to sea in fishing boats.

Isle of Harris

TOE HEAD

Soft green-brown in the morning sun,
Curled up and resting beside the blue-green sea
Like the old sheepdog
At the crofter's door.
The hunched back of the hills is
Clearly silhouetted against the pale sky.
Colours everchanging on the silent slopes
As the cloud-studded sky
Throws dark patches of shadow,
Ever moving, playing on the hills.
Toe Head becomes a giant chameleon,
Waiting and watching, its eye on the restless sea.
Turning purple in the brightness of the day
As the heather stretches towards the sun,
Rippling in shades and hues,
The wind whipping up its coat
Studded with white, woolly sheep –
Constantly moving.
As the evening paints the sky
In a kaleidoscope of colour,
With billowing spheres of cloud,
Toe Head stands towering, black
In dramatic pose,
Blotting out the sun,
Casting its shadow across Scarista bay.

Isle of Harris

THE FERRY PILGRIMS

As the ferry boat
Wearily sets out from Harris,
Threading its way through
A paradise of deserted islands,
A commotion of activity begins.
Gulls of many kinds
Rise up from their watery rest,
Wheeling over the rails
To float suspended
On invisible strings
In formation
Above the stern of the boat.
Looking down with quizzical eyes
At the amused passengers,
Watching keenly
For each discarded crumb.
Boldly they swerve and dive,
Snatching morsels from outstretched hands,
Strutting arrogantly along the deck rail,
Demanding attention.
Long, monotonous cries
Issue forth from curving throats,
Heads thrown back
For the final, piercing note
As the gulls alight on the mast –
Only to be pushed off by another
Uttering a victorious cry.
Like silent kites they glide,
Almost touching wingtips.
Feathers curved in sleek beauty,
Masters of the elements,
Defying the movement of ship and sea –
Hovering in apparent stillness,
Hypnotising the observer.
The moment is shattered

By a lightning dive
For food thrown seaward.
Yet in the scrabble
The scavenging crowd
Never touch or collide
In their eager flight,
Changing speed in a manner
That deceives the eye.
Once again they are overhead,
Hanging like a great mobile
Of elegant curves, suspended.
Graceful beauty, magnetised
By the ferry's turbulent wake.
The optimistic and insatiable
Ferry pilgrims.

THE BAT

Circling on scalloped wings,
Vibrating in the whirr of flight,
Rising, falling, spiralling –
Yet ever circling
In stammering curves.
Jerking, fluttering
In figures of eight,
Diving and arcing,
Orbiting the dusk of the garden
In timeless motion.
Darting silhouette
Beneath darkening skies,
Aimless, endless circling,
Shrouding the garden in mystery.
Master of the night
Surveying his domain,
Patrolling vigilantly –
Never tiring of circling
Clockwise and anti-clockwise
Over and over again
Until all the colours in the garden
Are absorbed into blackness.
Yet still he flutters
Over the well-worn flight track
Until he merges
Into the sleeping sky
And the world becomes a shadow
Of silent apprehension.

Is he still there –
Circling,
Pursuing his endless, untold mission?

WHO AM I?

When I analyse my experiences and my life, and consider the emotions I have felt, I know that the important thing is my attitude to life and other people as a result of my experiences and observations. All the time we are trying to find out who we really are and the meaning of our lives as we integrate with others. This search for our real identity is like an obstacle course that offers many choices and pitfalls. It is not the running of the course, but how we deal with it and our attitude that is so important. My quest for the answer to 'who am I?' leads me in many directions.

I am an ordinary, imperfect member of the human race. I see myself and others primarily as children of God.

I strive to be worthy of that label through the difficult task of moulding my nature to reflect God's attitude to mankind; that is, I strive to become a vessel of love.

This means breaking down the prejudices of centuries, locked within myself. I try not to see race, colour, creed, position or class, but to see firstly a fellow human being. By nature we humans are selfish, we want things for ourselves, to please ourselves. We conduct our lives around our own needs and desires, spending much of our time making a world of our own.

We let in only those who enhance our selfishness, who help us to build a better environment, or who fulfil one of our many needs, thus making our lives both satisfactory and enjoyable – but centred on ourselves.

If during this process of self-satisfaction others also find our environment enjoyable, then the situation is enhanced – we think we have found happiness, sometimes we call it love.

We allow very little compromise, we humans. Providing that our friends are enhancing our little personal world, all is well. If they assert themselves for any desires or needs of their own, producing attitudes or behaviour that unbalance our happy little world, then we challenge them. We discard or reject the situation and often the person.

Life is a constant struggle to keep the balance and hold together the cocoon of our personal world that we cherish so much. Any attempt to disrupt our little world is dealt with in no uncertain terms, by the selfish side of our nature, with protests, harsh words, hatred and violence. If we cannot retaliate, then we withdraw into a haze of self-pity as we try to patch up and remake the environment, centred on ourselves.

I understand that this inherited behaviour centred on myself is responsible for the miserable world I find myself in – societies and countries torn apart by strong, selfish individuals bent on creating their own world, at any cost, both to others and the natural environment.

If I am a child of God, my nature is in contradiction, so I need to strive to break down my selfish behaviour pattern as an individual as the first step towards creating a better world.

I need to centre myself on the needs and desires of others when building my own personal world – sacrificing my own needs and desires, thus breaking down my own selfish attitude. I exchange my own self-centred satisfaction for a new satisfaction, that is, pleasing others, creating harmony. Energy is concentrated on other people's happiness, centring on their world, not my own, trying to see life through their eyes not mine, and trying to understand other people's attitudes and fulfil their needs.

Who am I? Not the physical form you see, but the inner person, who thinks, acts, behaves and grows in a spiritual way. The real person is moulded by ourselves.

Because by nature we are selfish it is a hard struggle to change and become a child of God. Unfortunately, those enveloped by a self-centred nature have no qualms about using and taking advantage of those souls struggling for spiritual growth. This is part of the obstacle course of life. It should not deter one, but each situation should be a challenge to make positive strides to create unselfish attitudes.

In the quest to rid oneself of self-centred shackles, one grows beyond external trappings and material worldly values. One's vision becomes clearer and differences melt away. Age, infirmity, colour, race and position in our society are no longer barriers between friendships and communications. Understanding and compassion become more visible and more inviting. The world is created by internal values, not external, and the law of give and take becomes a balancing factor as self-sacrifice is equalised by mutual satisfactions.

To overcome self-centred behaviour one needs self-discipline to accept a challenging set of values and attempt to live by them.

If we can be devoid of all prejudice and develop a loving understanding of the nature and value of our fellow man, then we are nearer to building an ideal society.

Who am I? I am an ordinary imperfect human being with an ideal, a purpose in life. That purpose is to strive for my ideal, despite the frustrating temptations and difficulties that have to be overcome by my own nature. I may become disheartened, hurt, worn down and weary. It is often easier to give up the struggle and become self-centred, but that does not lead to true happiness. It takes a determined effort to keep your feet on the path to unconditional love, but what a paradise we would have if everyone managed to tread this path.

INDEX

afternoon in the Dales, An 108
Another time, another place 93
Anxiety 81
Awakening 103
Awareness 122

bat, The 152
Beginnings 99
Behold my Master 51
Benediction 117
blade of grass, A 33
breath of love, The 100
bridle path in winter, The 137
Brooke Churchyard 141
Butterfly 64

Changes 112
Confession 57
Continuation . . . 116
Cormorants 142
Cry wolf 80

Death of a cat 91

England 114
Equine spirit 32

ferry pilgrims, The 150
Fingal's Cave 144
Fionnphort 144
forgotten ones, The 128
Freedom 84

Garden colours 133
Give and take 30
Giving 50
Glensanda 146
Good friends 23
Grow your own love 75

Harvest rhythm 7
Hope 41
Hymn to Wales 109

I am nothing 10
In memory of a friend 90
In Nature's arms I rest 89
In sympathy with a sea anemone 85
Island peace 121
Isle of Eriska 145
Isle of Harris 121

Jean McCleod 126
Journey from Stornoway 147

Lament of a tennis widow 28
Learning 86
Learning to love 35
Light in the darkness 102
Love aborted 12
Love is . . . 2
Love is fragile 68
Love is giving 11
Love is green 132
Love lost 92
Love the sculptor 6
Love unveiled 10

Magic 12

man in the park, The 40
Man is a thief 70
Marble Quarry, Iona, The 110
Memories 98
Missing you 15
Morning greeting 107
Morning light, Lake Coniston 65
most precious things in life, The 29
My love for you 101

Neglected heart 32
new beginning, A 48
new era, A 25
New love 16

Oasis in rejection 38
observer, The 74

Pain 122
Paradise 135
path to love, The 13
Prayer 45

quality of life, The 76

Rain in the Dales 139
Reach out for me 39
Remember me 90
Remembrance 94
Restlessness 56
Romantic interlude 19

Scarista 148
search, The 78
secret place, A 108
Seeds of love 46
Sharing love 18
shell lives on, The 95
Signs of Spring 129
S.O.S. 28
Spider's web 59
Spiritual strength 44
Struggle 60

tangled mind of a mentally disturbed woman, The 62
Tarn Hows 115
Teacher retiring 24
Thinking of you 83
Think two 71
This man that I love 22
Thoughts from Hollie 96
Time on the beach 113
To be loved 73
Toe Head 149
Trust 80

Unconditional love 27
Under your spell 17
Unrivalled treasure 52

View from a hospital window 125
view beyond my pain, The 123

waters of life, The 46
Who cares? 36
wings of freedom, The 97
Words 6

X-ray, The 127

Yorkshire walls 138